Science 4
Learning Coach Guide

Part 1

About K12 Inc.

K12 Inc., a technology-based education company, is the nation's leading provider of proprietary curriculum and online education programs to students in grades K–12. K¹² provides its curriculum and academic services to online schools, traditional classrooms, blended school programs, and directly to families. K12 Inc. also operates the K¹² International Academy, an accredited, diploma-granting online private school serving students worldwide. K¹²'s mission is to provide any child the curriculum and tools to maximize success in life, regardless of geographic, financial, or demographic circumstances. K12 Inc. is accredited by CITA. More information can be found at www.K12.com.

Table of Contents

Unit 5: The Human Body

Learning Coach Guide
Lesson 1: Ecosystems and the Environment

In some way, every living thing on Earth depends on other living things, as well as on the nonliving parts of its environment. Explore the interactions among different organisms and their environment, and diagram these relationships using food chains and food webs. Find out how the sun's energy drives cycles in nature.

All over our planet, living things interact with other living things and also with nonliving things. *Ecology* is the study of these interactions. Discover how both living and nonliving things make up *ecosystems,* and how all of Earth's ecosystems make up one giant ecosystem--the *biosphere*.

Lesson Objectives

- Explore concepts to be addressed during the year in Science 4.
- Identify both living and nonliving parts of an ecosystem.
- Define a *population* as a group of individuals of the same type that live in a particular area.
- Define a *community* as a group of all the populations that live and interact with each other in a particular area.
- Describe how organisms depend on each other for survival, such as using each other as sources for food and shelter.

PREPARE

Approximate lesson time is 60 minutes.

Advance Preparation

- It's important that you read the Course Introduction for Science 4 before your student begins the course. You can find the course introduction at the beginning of the Ecosystems and the Environment lesson.
- It's important that you read the course introduction for Science 4th Grade before starting this lesson. You can find it by clicking the OLS "Help" section.

Materials

 For the Student
  binder, 3-ring
  paper, ruled
  pencil

Lesson Notes

All day long we interact with plants and animals. From eating a bowl of cereal to walking the dog to just smelling the flowers, even when we feel we are doing "nothing" we are interacting with our environment. We also interact with nonliving things. We feel the warmth of the sun and it motivates us to take a walk. A chilly breeze sends us back home to avoid the rain.

- *Ecology* is the study of the interactions between organisms and their environment.
- An *organism* is any living thing that takes in food, grows, and reproduces.

The environment, then, has both a living and a nonliving part. The nonliving part includes such things as temperature, sunlight, and the presence or absence of water. The living part includes all the other organisms with which an organism interacts.

Organisms can change the living part of their environments, as is done, for example, every time an owl swoops down and catches a field mouse. Organisms can also change the nonliving part of their environment. Earthworms, simply by making their way through the soil, help aerate the soil and, in turn, aerated soil helps plants grow. Thus, the earthworm has interacted with both the living and nonliving elements of its environment.

- Each individual is a member of a population.
- Together, populations form a community.

All the living things in a community depend on each other. The owl needs the mouse in order to stay alive. The flower needs the earthworm. Organisms also depend on the nonliving part of their environment. They all need energy from the sun, and they all need water from a pond, a stream, or the rain.

- An *ecosystem* is a community of organisms interacting with one another and with their environment.

Knowing where an organism lives gives us information about the organism itself. Different environments and, in particular, different climates allow different kinds of organisms to flourish.

- The Earth has three major climate zones: polar, temperate, and tropical.
- A *biome* is a large ecosystem with a community of animals and plants all living in the same climate.
- Each biome has different kinds of plants and animals living in it.

In the end, all biomes are subsumed under the largest ecosystem of all--the entirety of life on Earth. Earth's ecosystem is known as the *biosphere,* and it stretches from underground rocks, where bacteria may thrive, to the bottom of the oceans, where deep-sea fish live, to the highest mountain peak and above--high up into the air where the birds soar. If we discover that there is life elsewhere in the galaxy, we will perhaps need a larger category still. But at our present state of knowledge, Earth's biosphere is the grand community that unifies all others.

Keywords and Pronunciation

biome (BIY-ohm) : A large area with a distinctive community of animals and plants and a particular climate. The tundra is a biome that covers a large area of the northern part of the continents in the northern hemisphere.

biosphere (BIY-uh-sfir) : The entire portion of Earth inhabited by life. The Earth´s global ecosystem is called the biosphere, and it is the sum of all the planet's ecosystems.

climate : The usual pattern of weather that has occurred in an area over a long period of time. California's climate consists of hot, dry summers and mild, rainy winters.

community : All the populations that live and interact with each other in a particular area. Frogs, ducks, insects, and fish are some of the living things that help make up a pond community.

ecology : The study of the relationship between living things and their environment. A scientist studying a deer´s diet and shelter is studying ecology.

ecosystem (EE-koh-sis-tuhm) : A community of organisms interacting with one another and with their environment. Ecosystems can be large cities, vast jungles and forests, small tide pools, or even a terrarium.

environment (in-VIY-ruhn-muhnt) : The nonliving and living factors that affect an organism or community. The wind, water, soil, and interactions with other animals are all part of a rabbit's environment.

organism (OR-guhn-ih-zuhm) : Any living thing that takes in food, grows, and reproduces. Organisms are alive, a characteristic that makes them different from things such as rocks and water, which are not alive.

population : A group of individuals of the same type that live in a particular area. A large population of geese lives near that pond.

TEACH
Activity 1: Welcome to Science 4 *(Online)*
Instructions
Your student will navigate through a Course Introduction to learn about the organization and lesson layout of K12 Science 4. The interactive Course Introduction will explain the different kinds of lessons offered—from online science exploration, to offline science investigations and assessments. Join your student in navigating the Course Introduction for an orientation of this year's Science course.

Activity 2: Ecosystems and the Environment *(Online)*
Instructions
Have your student read through the Explore on his own. Reinforce and explain difficult concepts as needed.
Explore Suggestions:
Screen 7
Have your student draw the circles similar to the illustration on Screen 7. Starting with the smallest circle, write these terms in the circles in this order: individual, population, community, ecosystem, biome, and biosphere. Have your student define each term as he reads the Explore text.
After this activity, check to see if your student can:

- Identify both living and nonliving parts of an ecosystem.
- Define a population as a group of individuals of the same type that live in a particular area.
- State that a community is made up of all the populations that live and interact with each other in a particular area.
- Describe how organisms depend on each other for survival, such as using each other for food and shelter.

If your student has difficulty with any of these concepts, review the Explore with him and have him explain the key points on each screen.

Activity 3: The World Around You *(Online)*
Instructions
In this activity, your student will be asked to observe the world around him and describe the living and nonliving components. Allow him to think for himself as he responds to the questions below. These questions are also delivered directly to him in the Student portion of the lesson.

Have the student write answers on a piece of notebook paper under the following four headings: INDIVIDUAL, POPULATION, COMMUNITY, and ECOSYSTEM. Make sure your student writes his name, the date, and the lesson title on the paper. When he has finished, have him place his work into his Science Notebook.

After this activity, check to see if your student can:

- Identify both living and nonliving parts of an ecosystem.
- Define a *population* as a group of individuals of the same type that live in a particular area.
- State that a *community* is made up of all the populations that live and interact with each other in a particular area.
- Describe how organisms depend on each other for survival, such as serving as food and shelter.

ASSESS

Lesson Assessment: Ecosystems and Environment (*Offline*)

Students will complete an offline assessment based on the lesson objectives. Print the assessment and have students complete it on their own. Use the answer key to score the assessment, and then enter the results online. The attached answer key is the most current and may not coincide with previously printed guides.

Name _____   **Date** _____

Assessment

1. Draw an individual organism.

> **The drawing should show a single organism of any kind.**

2. Draw the same organism in a population.

> **The drawing should show a group of the same organism as in number 1.**

3. Draw a community of organisms. Be sure to include individuals from number 1.

> **The drawing should show several populations, plant or animal, including the population in number 2.**

Assessment

4. Choose one set of organisms from the list below and write at least two sentences describing how they interact and depend on each other for survival.

bird-tree
grass-zebra

bird - tree: Birds find shelter in trees as they build their nests and raise their young. Birds also eat the

fruit on trees and then spread the seeds to new places in their droppings. The droppings provide a

ready-made source of fertilizer for the germinating seeds.

grass - zebra: Zebras eat the grass. Zebras spread the grass seeds to new locations in their droppings

as they move with their herd.

5. Read the following description and list five nonliving parts of the cow's environment.

A cow leans down to take a drink of water from the cool stream. The cow turns and walks back up the stream's muddy bank to the herd of cows and one goat grazing on the green grass of the pasture. The animals swish their tails to shoo away the pesky flies. As the temperature rises on this hot afternoon, the cow wanders over to rest in the shade of a tree. A light breeze blows up and the sky darkens as clouds move across the sky, hiding the sun. A gentle rain falls and forms puddles in the cow path to the barn. Soon afterward the sky clears and the sun dries up the puddles.

1. _____ Answers should include Five of the following: water, stream, mud (or muddy

2. _____ bank), air temperature, shade, breeze (wind), sky (or air), clouds, rain, sun, ☐

3. _____ puddles.

4. _____

5. _____

Learning Coach Guide
Lesson 2: Producers, Consumers, and Decomposers

From the tallest tree to the tiniest speck of bacteria, organisms called *producers, consumers,* and *decomposers* are constantly recycling nutrients that all organisms need to survive. Find out where you fit in this process. Then do an experiment and watch some common household waste decompose to become food for plants.

Lesson Objectives

- State that all organisms need some source of energy to live.
- Distinguish between *herbivores, carnivores,* and *omnivores* according to their diets.
- Identify examples of producers, consumers, and decomposers.
- Describe the roles of *producers, consumers,* and *decomposers* in an ecosystem.
- Describe how nutrients are continuously recycled through an ecosystem among producers, consumers, and decomposers.

PREPARE

Approximate lesson time is 60 minutes.

Materials

For the Student

    bottle, plastic - 1 - liter, top removed

    household item - bread

    household item - eggshells

    household item - fruit peel

    household item - lettuce leaves

    household item - newspaper

    paper, ruled

    soil

    aluminum foil

    paper, notebook - small strip

    pencil

    plastic wrap

    ruler

    scissors

    spoon

    tape, masking

    grass clippings

    household item - container with lid

    household item - large container with lid

    waste, kitchen

    shovel

Lesson Notes

Every living thing needs energy, and this fact raises the immediate question of where organisms get the energy they need to live. The source of energy for all living thing things is food. Many organisms eat living or recently living things. Plants get their energy from the sun. Some animals eat plants. Some animals get their energy from other animals. If a deer is killed and eaten by a wolf, the energy that the wolf needs to survive is taken from the deer. In other words, the energy the deer got from eating plants was stored in its body, and the energy the wolf gets from eating the deer is then stored in its body. Energy gets passed from organism to organism.

Producers and Consumers

How, then, does the whole process get started? The answer is in the sun. Plants convert solar energy--sunlight--into food through the process of photosynthesis.

Because plants can produce their own food, they are called *producers*. Organisms that depend on other organisms for food are called *consumers*. The deer is a consumer--it eats grass, taking energy from the plant. The wolf is a consumer--it eats the deer.

Scientists distinguish between different consumers based on their diets. An *herbivore* eats plants. A *carnivore* eats other animals. An *omnivore* eats both plants and animals.

Not all carnivores hunt down and kill their food, though. Some simply wait until others have done the killing, and then grab a quick meal off the carcass. Carnivores that do this are called *scavengers*. They scavenge off dead bodies. The wolf does not entirely consume the deer, but leaves plenty of it behind. What is left provides the energy for other living things.

Decomposers

Even after scavengers have "picked clean" a body, there is still more energy to be gotten as the body rots or decomposes. *Decomposers* are consumers that get their energy from organic material, such as dead leaves, fallen branches, and the remains of animals and plants.

Fungi (mushrooms and molds), insects, earthworms, and bacteria are all decomposers that break down organic material and recycle nutrients back into the soil, water, and air.

The process of decomposition is an entirely natural sequence of events. It is merely part of the cycle by which energy is passed from living thing to living thing. Decomposers also connect the living and nonliving parts of the environment as they recycle the chemicals that make up all living organisms.

Energy and Nutrient Cycling

Thus the whole arrangement begins with the sun, which puts out energy all the time. Producers catch the sunlight and turn it into food. Herbivores eat the leaves, fruit, vegetables, and such of the producers. Carnivores may eat the herbivores. Scavengers clean off the remains, and then decomposers return the last of the elements to the ground. This final process enriches the soil with nutrients, making possible the growth of new producers.

The same nutrients are constantly recycled within and among ecosystems. Decomposers break down organic material and recycle the nutrients back into the environment.

If your student asks where the sun gets its energy, congratulate him on smart thinking. The answer in simple terms is that atomic reactions in the sun (called nuclear fusion) give off enormous amounts of energy including light. Most of these reactions involve the element hydrogen as the sun's "fuel." Is the sun using up its supply of hydrogen? Yes, but the sun contains so much hydrogen that it won't stop giving off energy for billions of years.

Keywords and Pronunciation

carnivore (KAHR-nuh-vor) : An animal that feeds mainly on other animals. A tiger is considered a carnivore since its diet is mainly other animals.

consumer : An organism that depends on other organisms for food. Consumers directly or indirectly depend on producers for their energy. A robin is a consumer that eats worms.

decomposers : those organisms that break down dead organic matter

ecosystem (EE-koh-sis-tuhm) : A community of organisms interacting with one another and with their environment. Ecosystems can be large cities, vast jungles and forests, small tide pools, or even a terrarium.

environment (in-VIY-ruhn-muhnt) : The nonliving and living factors that affect an organism or community. The wind, water, soil, and interactions with other animals are all part of a rabbit's environment.

herbivore (UR-buh-vor) : An animal that feeds mainly on plants. A cow is considered an herbivore since its diet is mainly plants.

omnivore (AHM-nih-vor) : An animal that eats both plants and animals. Bears are omnivores, and eat fruits, nuts, fish, and small animals.

photosynthesis (foh-toh-SINT-thuh-suhs)

producers : Organisms, such as plants or algae, that make (or produce) their own food. Plants produce their own food through the process of photosynthesis.

scavengers : An animal that eats the bodies of dead animals. A vulture is a scavenger.

TEACH
Activity 1: Energy in an Ecosystem *(Online)*
Instructions

Have your student read through the Explore on his own. Reinforce and explain difficult concepts as needed.

Explore Suggestions:

Screen 1: Use the illustration to help your student review the relationships between individuals, populations, communities, ecosystems, biomes, and the biosphere

Screen 3: The producers are: the leaves, grass, and lettuce on the table. The consumers are: the deer, fox, mouse, and the people sitting at the table.

Screen 6: Make sure your student understands how nutrients cycle throughout the ecosystem. Challenge him to develop examples of his own for each stage in the nutrient cycle. The exact organisms he chooses are not important, as long as he correctly identifies them as producers, consumers (herbivore, carnivore, omnivore), and decomposers.

After this activity, check to see if your student can:

- Identify both living and nonliving parts of an ecosystem.
- Define a *population* as a group of individuals of the same type that live in a particular area.
- State that a *community* is made up of all the populations that live and interact with each other in a particular area.
- Describe how organisms depend on each other for survival, such as using each other as sources for food and shelter.

If your student has difficulty with any of these concepts, review the Explore with him and have him explain the key points on each screen.

Activity 2: Decomposition Station (Offline)
Instructions

In this activity, your student will compare materials to see if they decompose. He should understand that what determines whether or not a material decomposes is whether it was once living (or was made from a living thing) or is nonliving. For example, paper is made from trees and will decompose. Aluminum foil is made from a mineral ore and will not decompose.

There may not be a significant amount of decomposition of the eggshells after only two weeks, additional time may be needed.

Guide your student to make and fill out a table to compare the materials. The table should consist of three columns and eight rows and completed as follows:

- Label the tops of the columns as follows: MATERIALS, PREDICTIONS, OBSERVATIONS.
- Then write the following list of objects under the MATERIALS column: paper, fruit peel, lettuce leaves, plastic wrap, aluminum foil, bread, egg.
- Predict which material will decompose or will not decompose. Write "yes" or "no" in the PREDICTIONS column next to the item.
- Keep your chart in your Science Notebook until you are ready to make your observations.

At the end of this activity, check to see if your student can:

- State that all organisms need some source of energy to live.
- Distinguish between herbivores, carnivores, and omnivores according to their diets.
- Identify examples of producers, consumers, and decomposers.
- Describe the roles of producers, consumers, and decomposers in an ecosystem.
- Describe how nutrients are continuously recycled through an ecosystem among producers, consumers, and decomposers.

ASSESS

Lesson Assessment: Producers, Consumers, and Decomposers (*Online*)

Students will complete an offline assessment based on the lesson objectives. Print the assessment and have students complete it on their own. Use the answer key to score the assessment, and then enter the results online. The attached answer key is the most current and may not coincide with previously printed guides.

TEACH

Activity 3. Optional: Make Your Own Compost Pile (*Online*)
Instructions

In this activity, your student can make a compost pile that can be used to help a backyard garden grow. Preparing a compost pile takes a considerable amount of time, but is a good alternative to just throwing kitchen waste away. Use caution that when making the compost pile that you do not use meat, butter, or oil. It will attract rats or other animals scavenging for food. Use a large container or trashcan with a lid in which to collect the compost materials. Inside the container, your student will alternate layers of soil with kitchen waste.

Safety

This lesson involves eating or working with food. Before beginning, check with your doctor, if necessary, to find out whether your student will have any allergic reaction to the food.

Lesson Assessment Answer Key

Producers, Consumers, and Decomposers

Answers.

1. C

2. A

3. B

4. tree and grass

5. grasshopper, frog, snake, caterpillar, monkey, fish

6. mold, mushrooms, bacteria

7. All living things decompose when they die.

8. Answer may vary, but should include that producers make food energy for themselves, but when they are eaten by animals, this food energy gets passed around.

9. Answer may vary, but should include that consumers are organisms that depend on other organisms for food, such as producers or other consumers.

10. Nutrients are constantly recycled within an ecosystem because decomposes break down things that were once living, such as fallen leaves, dead wood, animal droppings, and dead plants and animals and recycle the nutrients back into the environment.

11. true

12. true

13. The plant would die because all organisms need some source of energy to live.

Learning Coach Guide
Lesson 3: Food Webs: Energy Flow in an Ecosystem

Have you ever heard someone say, "You are what you eat"? Believe it or not, the food you eat provides you with energy from the sun! Find out how this happens as you use food chains, food webs, and energy pyramids to show how food and energy get passed through ecosystems.

Lesson Objectives

- State that sunlight is the original source of energy for almost all ecosystems and therefore, all life.
- Explain how a *food web* combines food chains to show the interconnected feeding relationships in an ecosystem.
- Explain how a *food chain* shows the pathway along which food is transferred from one organism to another.
- Recognize that an *energy pyramid* is a diagram that shows the amount of energy available at each level of an ecosystem.
- Recognize that energy is lost as you move up through levels of the energy pyramid.

PREPARE

Approximate lesson time is 60 minutes.

Advance Preparation

- For the Beyond the Lesson activity, set up the vivarium first, then purchase the anole and crickets from a pet store.

Materials

For the Student

📖 Food Chains and Webs Pattern Sheet

household item - newspaper

pencil

scissors

string - or yarn

anole

carrot

cricket, live

household item - cling film

household item - knife

household item - masking tape

household item - oatmeal

plant

plastic bottle - 2-litre

soil

apple

rocks

water

Lesson Notes

All living things need energy to grow, energy to reproduce, energy to survive. All ecosystems, therefore, need energy. Their energy begins with the sun. Plants trap the solar energy and, through photosynthesis, convert it into the sugars that are their food. Animals eat the plants, taking some of that sun-harvested energy into themselves. Other animals eat those animals.

Eventually, the animals die. Their bodies are cleaned off by scavengers and dismantled by decomposers. The remaining minerals are returned to the soil, which is enriched by them so that it is once again fertile and can support new plants. Around and around it goes.

These relationships--which organisms eat which other organisms, and how the energy is passed from one to another--can be thought of in terms of an imaginary chain. In this chain, each organism forms a single link: the chain stretches from the blackberries to the mouse that eats one to the owl that catches the mouse. Such an imaginary chain is known as a *food chain*. Food chains describe the flow of energy, in the form of food, from one organism to another. Each organism forms a link in the chain.

Almost all food chains begin with producers harvesting energy from the sun. From there the energy is passed from producers to consumers: herbivores, carnivores, and omnivores. When these die the energy passes to scavengers and decomposers, and back into the soil. Decomposers, as the last step to replenishing the soil, are both the end and the beginning of any food chain.

We can see that, as with a real chain, removing any link causes the entire chain to collapse. If the plants were removed, for example, it would not simply affect herbivores--for carnivores eat the herbivores. If the decomposers were removed, the soil would not become replenished with minerals; new plants would not grow; herbivores would not feed on them. And if the sun were removed from the chain--perhaps by pollution blocking its light--nothing else on the chain would remain. The last living recipient of energy in a food chain is called the *top consumer*. It will not be consumed itself until it dies.

Food chains are a helpful way to think about how energy moves through an ecosystem. In any real situation, though, there are many different food chains, all connected to each other. A *food web* is a diagram that combines food chains to show these connections. Food webs are made of interconnected food chains.

These relationships can also be imagined as a pyramid, with plants on the bottom, then herbivores, and then carnivores. This kind of diagram is known as an *energy pyramid.*

Energy is lost between every feeding level of an energy pyramid. Only about one-tenth of the energy in plants flows to herbivores. One-tenth of the energy in herbivores flows to carnivores. The rest is used up in the process of staying alive or lost as heat.

The most abundant organisms in any ecosystem, aside from the decomposers, will be the producers. Plants have the most energy available to them because they trap it directly from the sun. There will be fewer carnivores and even fewer top carnivores. Small populations of top carnivores depend on much larger populations of other animals to survive.

Keywords and Pronunciation

carnivore (KAHR-nuh-vor) : An animal that feeds mainly on other animals. A tiger is considered a carnivore since its diet is mainly other animals.

energy : The ability of living things to live, grow, move, and reproduce. Plants get their energy from the sun. Animals get their energy by eating plants and other animals.

energy pyramid : a diagram that shows the amount of energy available at each trophic level of a food chain; the level of a food chain that has the most energy available is the producers, the largest part of the energy pyramid; also called an energy flow or productivity pyramid

food chain : The pathway along which food is transferred from one organism to another. A worm eats a leaf, then a bird eats the worm, then an owl eats the bird. This is an example of a food chain.

food web : A diagram that combines food chains to show the interconnected feeding relationships in an ecosystem. Plants and animals can be part of more than one food chain in a food web.

herbivore (UR-buh-vor) : An animal that feeds mainly on plants. A cow is considered an herbivore since its diet is mainly plants.

omnivore (AHM-nih-vor) : An animal that eats both plants and animals. Bears are omnivores, and eat fruits, nuts, fish, and small animals.

vivarium (viy-VAIR-ee-uhm)

TEACH
Activity 1: Where Does the Energy Go? *(Online)*

Instructions
Have your student read through the Explore on his own. Reinforce and explain difficult concepts as needed.

Explore Suggestions:

Screen 2
Why is the term food chain a good way to describe the relationship between how organisms depend on each other for food? Have your student relate links in a real chain to links in a food chain.

Screen 4
Before your student uses the interactive food web, have him try to identify a few of the food chains in the web. He can then see if he is correct.

Screen 6
The process by which plants trap energy from the sun to produce their own food is called photosynthesis. Ask your student why photosynthesis is important to all living things? (All consumers, either directly or indirectly, rely on the food energy made by producers.)

Have your student make a sketch of the energy pyramid.

After this activity, check to see if your student can:

- State that sunlight is the original source of energy for almost all ecosystems and therefore all life.
- Explain how a food chain shows the pathway along which food is transferred from one organism to another.
- Explain how a food web combines food chains to show the interconnected feeding relationships in an ecosystem.
- Recognize that an energy pyramid is a diagram that shows the amount of energy available at each level of an ecosystem.
- Recognize that energy is lost as you move up through levels of the energy pyramid.

If your student is having difficulty with any of these concepts, review the Explore with him and have him explain the key points on each screen.

Activity 2: Chains, Webs, and Pyramids *(Offline)*
Instructions
In this activity, your student will use the cards from the Food Chains and Webs Pattern Sheet to sort the organisms into groups of producers, herbivores, carnivores, and omnivores. He will then use the same cards to form food chains. Finally, he will see how all of the food chains interconnect to form a food web.

As your student works through the activity:
- Check to make sure your student correctly sorts the animals into groups of producers, herbivores, carnivores, and omnivores.
  Producers: algae, water lily, and duckweed
  Herbivores: duck, daphnia, and snail
  Carnivores: frog, great blue heron, mink, dragonfly, fish
  Omnivore: turtle

- Have your student explain the difference between a food chain and a food web. Emphasize that most organisms eat more than one thing, and food webs show many interconnected food pathways.
  Examples of food chains:

  algae-daphnia-frog-great blue heron or mink or turtle

  duckweed-turtle-mink

  water lily-snail-frog-great blue heron or mink or turtle

- Have your student choose a food chain and explain how energy is transferred through an ecosystem.
- Ask him questions such as:
  - What is the original source of energy for all the food chains you have made? (the sun)
  - Which animals have the most energy available to them to use? (producers: algae, water lily, duckweed)
  - Which animals have the least amount of energy to use? (consumers [carnivores] at the top of the food chain, such as great blue herons, mink)
  - Ask your student in what type of ecosystem might he find all these animals? (pond)

ASSESS

Lesson Assessment: Food Webs: Energy Flow in an Ecosystem (*Online*)

Students will complete an offline assessment based on the lesson objectives. Print the assessment and have students complete it on their own. Use the answer key to score the assessment, and then enter the results online. The attached answer key is the most current and may not coincide with previously printed guides.

TEACH

Activity 3. Optional: Make an Ecosystem! (*Online*)

Instructions

In this activity, your student will be making a vivarium to create a small ecosystem. He will be able to observe the organisms within the vivarium and see how they interact with each other. Once the vivarium is in place, allow your student to observe it for a week.

He should notice that the anole eats the crickets and the crickets eat the oatmeal, carrots, and apples. If conditions are right, fungus (mold) and bacteria will begin to grow on the remains of the oatmeal, carrots, and apples, completing the nutrient cycling and beginning it again.

Note: Making and keeping a vivarium is exciting but requires some time and resources. You may wish to read more about the care of anoles and reptiles before beginning this activity with your child at Care Sheet and Lizard Care Sheet. Instead of an anole, you may wish to choose another lizard such as a gecko.

Anoles live approximately 2 to 5 years in captivity. The vivarium in this activity is contained in a plastic 2-liter bottle. If you have a small 10 gallon aquarium with a screened top, use that instead of the bottle. Anoles only eat live food, so you will need to continue purchasing small crickets, mealworms, or waxworms for your pet anole. Consult with your local pet store and veterinarian about specific feeding instructions for your pet. Anoles naturally spend time in trees and drink by lapping water from leaves and will not drink from a cup of water. Be sure you sprinkle or spray the leaves with water daily. Plants with broad leaves are preferable because anoles can more easily perch on them. If there is room in the vivarium, place a stick inside for the anole to rest on.

You will need to add very small pieces of fresh carrots and apples for the crickets to feed on.

Answers:

[1] producers: plants (oatmeal, carrots, and apple); consumers: anole and crickets; decomposers: mold and bacteria

[2] anole, crickets, plant, mold, and bacteria that may be growing

[3] rock, soil, water, air, oatmeal, carrots, apple

[4] The anole will eat the cricket, oatmeal, carrot, and apple. The plant will use the nutrients from the soil and water to grow. Fungus (mold) or bacteria may grow on the soil, and on the remains of the carrot and apple.

Lesson Assessment

Food Webs: Energy Flow in an Ecosystem

Answers:

1. grass, grasshopper, frog, snake, hawk

2. Owl. The smallest portion of the energy reaches the top of the pyramid, and the owl is at the top..

3. Grass and oak tree. The grass and the oak tree are producers. Producers have the most amount of the sun's energy available to them.

4. Most organisms eat more than one thing.

5. sun

Learning Coach Guide
Lesson 4: Cycles in Ecosystems

Nature does not waste anything. Water and nutrients recycle through the environment to provide the food, air, and water that living things need. Study the water and carbon cycles to discover how they keep nutrient levels in balance, and how humans can sometimes alter the balance by causing these cycles to change.

Lesson Objectives

- Recognize that cycles in nature provide organisms with the food, air, and water they need to live, grow, and reproduce.
- Describe how water continuously moves through the water cycle as it evaporates, condenses, and precipitates.
- Identify the ways carbon is cycled through both living (organic) and nonliving (inorganic) parts of an ecosystem.
- Use the greenhouse effect to explain how humans have caused a change in the carbon cycle.

PREPARE

Approximate lesson time is 60 minutes.

Materials

For the Student

    📖 The Water Cycle/Carbon Cycle Connection

    crayons, 64 colors or more

    paper, notebook

    pencil

    📖 The Greenhouse Effect

    jar - with lid

    soil

    thermometer (2)

For the Adult

    📖 The Water Cycle/Carbon Cycle Connection Answer Key

Lesson Notes

With a few rare exceptions, all the energy for life on Earth comes from the sun. The sun is an almost unlimited energy source--it never stops pouring energy in the form of light down onto the Earth. Ecosystems that use sunlight never run out of light energy, but ecosystems can run out of nutrients. A *nutrient* is a chemical compound that organisms need to stay alive.|

This lesson discusses two cycles: the water cycle and the carbon cycle. Water is not technically a nutrient, but the principles of its circulation are the same as those for nutrient cycling.

In the *water cycle,* water on the land evaporates into the air and condenses into clouds and precipitation. Precipitation falls from the clouds and may form streams or puddles on the land. The water runs into the ground or into rivers, and the rivers run into the sea. Water in the sea evaporates once more into the air. The cycle continues.

In the *carbon cycle,* carbon moves through an ecosystem. Carbon is an essential element in all organic matter. Examples of carbon compounds that are nutrients are carbon dioxide, sugars, and starches. *Organic matter* is matter that comes from organisms, living or dead. *Inorganic matter* does not come from organisms. Stones, for example, are inorganic matter.

Carbon moves in a cycle through both types of matter. Some forms of carbon are useable, but not others. The carbon in coal, for example, is not in a chemical form that plants can take up. The nutrients containing carbon in grass, such as cellulose or sugars, are readily available, and can be consumed by animals. The illustration on screen 3 helps clarify this distinction.

Like the water cycle, the carbon cycle has a natural balance. Humans can change that balance when they introduce too much carbon into one place while removing it from another. A good example of how we change natural cycles is the greenhouse effect.

Light energy from the sun warms the Earth. Most of the heat from the sunlight bounces off the planet and heads back into space. Some of it stays and keeps the planet warm enough for life. That is due to the normal greenhouse effect. If the incoming heat from the sun meets too much carbon dioxide on the way back up, however, it may bounce back down again--the heat energy is unable to escape. This extra heat could makes the Earth gradually grow hotter and hotter, a condition that could give rise to potentially devastating climate changes. Many scientists now see evidence that an excess of carbon dioxide in our atmosphere, in part the result of human-generated carbon dioxide, is enhancing the normal greenhouse function of the atmosphere.

Keywords and Pronunciation

inorganic : Matter that does not come from an animal or plant. Rocks and minerals are inorganic.

organic : Matter that comes from an animal or plant and contains carbon. Leaves, whether alive or dead, are organic.

TEACH
Activity 1: The Earth's Natural Cycles *(Online)*
Instructions

Have your student read through the Explore on his own. Reinforce and explain difficult concepts as needed.

Explore Suggestions:

Screen 3: Explain that coal, oil, and peat are useable, just not by living things as nutrients.

Screen 4: Explain that when humans exhale, they give off carbon dioxide. Nature balances out this carbon dioxide by plants, which take in carbon dioxide and give off oxygen. Humans do not harm the atmosphere by breathing out!

Screen 5: Have your student imagine he is a carbon atom in a banana peel. Where was he before he was present in the banana? What might happen to him next? Is it possible he might become a carbon atom in another banana? [Yes, as carbon from the peel could be recycled back into the soil then used by a nearby banana tree.]

Screen 6: Nature's cycles such as water and carbon cycles are balanced. Any changes that occur take place within limits that allow life to go on. Human activities can change the balance of these natural cycles.

After this activity, check to see if your student can:

- Recognize that cycles in nature provide organisms with the food, air, and water they need to live, grow, and reproduce.
- Describe how water continuously moves through the water cycle as it evaporates, condenses, and precipitates.

- Identify two ways carbon is cycled through both living (organic) and nonliving (inorganic) parts of an ecosystem.
- Use the greenhouse effect to explain how humans have caused a change in the carbon cycle.

If your student has difficulty with any of these concepts, you may wish to review the Explore with him and have him explain the key points on each screen.

Activity 2: The Water Cycle-Carbon Cycle Connection (Offline)
Instructions

In this activity, your student will be asked to label the steps in both the water and carbon cycles. He should understand that the cycles are continuous and never ending. He will also be asked to describe the ways that carbon becomes part of the Earth's atmosphere and how humans have contributed to the increase in carbon dioxide resulting in the greenhouse effect.

At the end of this activity, check to see if your student can:
- Describe how water continuously moves through the water cycle as it evaporates, condenses, and precipitates.
- Identify two ways carbon is cycled through both living (organic) and nonliving (inorganic) parts of an ecosystem.
- Use the greenhouse effect to explain how humans have caused a change in the carbon cycle.

ASSESS

Lesson Assessment: Cycles in Ecosystems (*Online*)

Students will complete an offline assessment based on the lesson objectives. Print the assessment and have students complete it on their own. Use the answer key to score the assessment, and then enter the results online. The attached answer key is the most current and may not coincide with previously printed guides.

TEACH

Activity 3. Optional: The Greenhouse Effect (Offline)
Instructions

In this activity, your student will make a model of the greenhouse effect using a jar with a lid, soil, and two thermometers.

Discuss with your student how the Earth is too large to observe the greenhouse effect all at once. Scientists make models to study such large-scale effects. In this activity, the jar is a small model of a greenhouse. Greenhouses are made of clear plastic or glass that allows energy from the sun to heat the plants inside. Because a greenhouse is closed, the cooler air outside does not mix with the warm air inside.

On Earth, the sun's light energy strikes the surface of the Earth and the surface gives off heat. Gases such as carbon dioxide trap the heat close to the Earth.

Name _____   Date _____

The Water Cycle / Carbon Cycle Connection

Carbon Cycle

Write the number next to the part of the picture that is described below. Then draw arrows in RED connecting each number to show the path of carbon in the carbon cycle.

1. During photosynthesis, plants use carbon dioxide from the air to make food.
2. Animals consume carbon when they eat plants.
3. Living organisms return carbon dioxide to the air when they breathe out.
4. Organisms die and decomposers release carbon into the soil, air, or water.
5. Some carbon is trapped for millions of years, forming coal and oil.
6. Factories burning coal and oil release carbon dioxide back into the air to be used by plants to make food.

Water Cycle

Write the letter next to the part of the picture that is described below. Then draw arrows in BLUE connecting each number to show the path of water in the water cycle.

A. Light energy from the sun evaporates water from oceans, rivers, ponds, and, lakes. The water becomes water vapor.
B. Water vapor in the atmosphere condenses to form clouds and precipitation.
C. Precipitation falls back to the Earth's surface.
D. Water seeps into the ground.
E. Water that cannot seep into the ground runs off the surface forming streams and rivers and filling up ponds and lakes to be evaporated again by the sun.

The Water Cycle / Carbon Cycle Connection

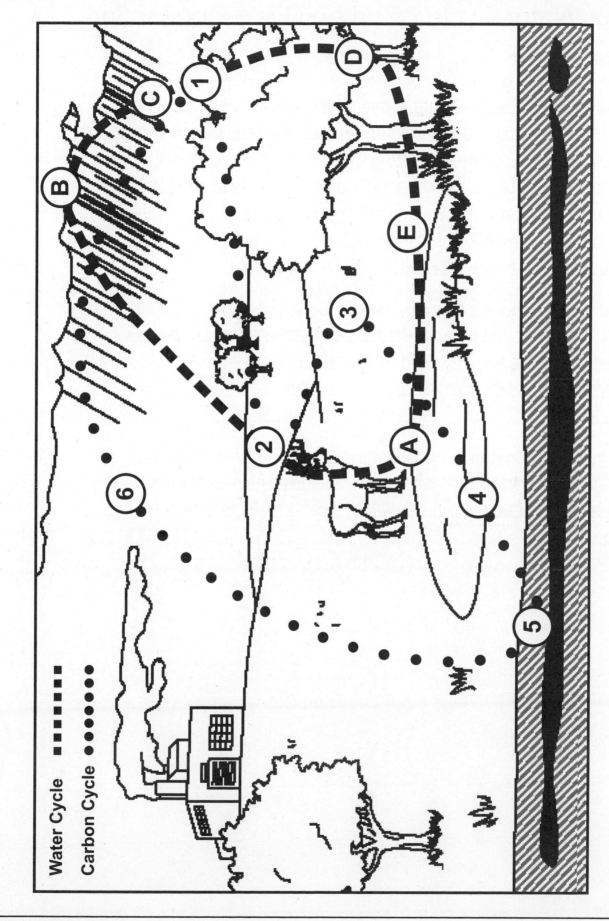

Water Cycle ▪▪▪▪▪ **Carbon Cycle** ●●●●●

23

The Water Cycle / Carbon Cycle Connection

Think About It

How does carbon dioxide on Earth act like the glass panes in a greenhouse? **Clear glass in a greenhouse lets the sun's light through but traps heat inside. On Earth, the sun's light energy passes through the atmosphere and hits the surface. Some of the sun's energy is reflected back from the surface as heat. Carbon dioxide and other gases can trap this heat inside the Earth's atmosphere. The air inside the Earth's atmosphere then becomes warmer than the air outside. This is called the greenhouse effect.**

In what ways does carbon dioxide become part of the Earth's atmosphere? **Animals naturally give off carbon dioxide when they exhale. Burning coal and oil in factories produces carbon dioxide, and it becomes part of the atmosphere.**

Tell how humans have changed the balance of carbon dioxide in the Earth's atmosphere. **Burning coal and oil in factories and cars has produced higher levels of carbon dioxide in the atmosphere.**

Lesson Assessment Answer Key

Cycles in Ecosystems

Answers:

1. Answer may include: Some carbon is trapped for millions of years, forming coal and oil. Factories burning coal and oil release carbon dioxide back into the air.
2. Answers my include the following: During photosynthesis, plants use carbon dioxide from the air to make food. Animals consume carbon when they eat plants. Living organisms return carbon dioxide to the air when they breathe out. Organisms die and decomposers release carbon into the soil, air, or water.
3. Your student should sketch the following stages of the water cycle: evaporation, condensation, precipitation, seepage, and runoff.
4. shelter
5. Burning fuels such as coal and oil creates higher levels of carbon dioxide in the air.

Learning Coach Guide
Lesson 5: Changing Environmental Conditions

Is there anything you can't live without? You might have a book or a bike you like very much, but if you didn't have them you would still be able to survive. Something in the environment that a living thing must have in order to survive--such as temperature, water, or air--is called a *limiting factor.* Think about your limiting factors as you learn about those of other organisms.

Lesson Objectives

- Recognize that conditions within an ecosystem are constantly changing, causing plants and animals to adapt, move, or die.
- Identify a *limiting factor* as any environmental condition that can reduce an organism's ability to survive (for example, changes in temperature and abundance of food, water, sunlight, and nutrients).
- State that organisms can live within a certain range of environmental conditions.
- Recognize that limiting factors can change from ecosystem to ecosystem and from organism to organism.

PREPARE

Approximate lesson time is 60 minutes.

Advance Preparation

- Print the Temperature Control Lab sheet. Assist your student with beginning the investigation. Stop just before the section labeled "Scientists' Notes". Review the procedure with your student when you teach the entire lesson.

- If you are using a pre-moistened sponge, 10 mL of water should be enough to moisten it for the experiment. If you are using a dry sponge, be sure to use the same amount of water to moisten each of the nine sponges.

Materials

For the Student

🖥 Temperature Control

birdseed - 1 cup

light bulb, 60 watt

sponge, kitchen (9)

bags, zipper-close (9)

lamp

markers - permanent

paper, construction, 9" x 12" - black (3)

pencil

ruler

scissors

water

📖 Too Hot!
> shovel
> thermometer - outdoor (2)
> towel - white

Lesson Notes

In past lessons, your student has learned that cycles exist in nature, such as the cycles that pass nutrients among the different living things in an ecosystem. The paths these nutrients take, however, depend on a few things:

- Type of nutrient
- Types of organisms
- Environmental conditions

In this lesson, we will be considering the factors, environmental conditions (such as temperature, water and air), and how they influence and are influenced by living things in an ecosystem.

- The environment determines what organism live there.

An environmental condition that limits an organism's ability to survive is called a *limiting factor*. Limiting factors are things such as the amount of sunlight in a region, the amount of water, and the kind of nutrients present in the soil.

Temperature is a good example of a limiting factor. Your student will understand that a polar bear is adapted to an extremely cold environment, and would not survive long on a tropical island. By the same token, a python would soon freeze in the polar bear's natural habitat.

Sunlight and water are limiting factors. If your student has ever seen a plant from a nursery, you could discuss the tag that explains what conditions (limiting factors) are needed for the plant's health. Some plants need shade, others sun; some need a lot of water, others very little.

Limiting factors can exist in the relationship between living things. Many trees depend on insects to germinate their blossoms. The fruit a tree produces is food for animals, and the animals spread the seeds. Impairing any part of this network, such as by removing the blossoms one season, affects all the other organisms as well.

Organisms can also compete for space or resources. In the example given in the Explore section of this lesson, pandas are running out of their food supply because humans are cutting down bamboo--the pandas' food source--to build houses.

Keywords and Pronunciation

limiting factor : An environmental condition that affects or limits the ability of an organism to survive. A limiting factor for an earthworm is the amount of water present in the ground.

photosynthesis (foh-toh-SINT-thuh-suhs)

TEACH
Activity 1: Environmental Changes *(Online)*
Instructions

Have your student read through the Explore on his own. Reinforce and explain difficult concepts as needed. Use examples of daily life to explain the nature of limiting factors. A plant, birds in the area, or even earthworms in a park can serve as a springboard for discussing factors that limit population size. Most limiting factors are obvious and usually boil down to food, shelter, water, and the availability of mates.

After this activity, check to see if your student can:
- Recognize that conditions within an ecosystem are constantly changing, causing plants and animals to adapt, move, or die.
- Identify a *limiting factor* as any environmental condition that can reduce the ability of an organism to survive, such as changes in temperature and abundance of food, water, sunlight, and nutrients.
- State that organisms can live within a certain range of environmental conditions.
- Recognize that limiting factors can change from ecosystem to ecosystem and from organism to organism.

If your student has difficulty with any of these concepts, you may wish to review the Explore with him and have him explain the key points on each screen.

Activity 2: Temperature Control *(Offline)*
Instructions

In this activity, your student will experiment with the limiting factor of temperature on seed growth. The seeds that were "planted" seven days ago should have begun to demonstrate whether or not they will grow in the various conditions you placed them in.

This may be your student's first time experimenting with independent and dependent variables. Read and discuss the Science Notes section of the lab sheet with him to see if he understands the concept. He should understand that placing a piece of construction paper over all the seeds rules out the variable of light.
Be sure to review the Procedure section of the lab sheet before your student begins making observations. Your student should find that the seeds placed in the freezer have not even begun to germinate. The cold temperature is not the best growing condition for some types of seeds. The seeds placed under the lamp may have the longest sprouts, followed by the seeds placed on the counter. The warmer environment provided by the heat of the lamp is a more ideal growing condition for some seeds. If your student's seeds do not yield the typical results, review the Science Notes section with him again and discuss what variables may have altered the findings (such as a stove near the seeds on the counter that produces more heat).
At the end of this activity, your student should be able to:
- Identify a *limiting factor* as any environmental condition that can reduce the ability of an organism to survive (for example, changes in temperature and abundance of food, water, sunlight, and nutrients).
- State that organisms can live within a certain range of environmental conditions.

Safety

The seeds and seedlings in the Temperature Control experiment may become mouldy. Use caution handling them if your student is allergic to mold.

ASSESS

Lesson Assessment: Changing Environmental Conditions (*Online*)

Students will complete an offline assessment based on the lesson objectives. Print the assessment and have students complete it on their own. Use the answer key to score the assessment, and then enter the results online. The attached answer key is the most current and may not coincide with previously printed guides.

TEACH

Activity 3. Optional: Too Hot! *(Online)*

Instructions

Temperature can be a limiting factor for the plants and animals of the desert. Many desert animals stay underground during the day to avoid the intense heat. Your student will perform an experiment to see just how much cooler the temperature is underground.

Lesson Assessment Answer Key

Changing Environmental Conditions

Answers:

1. limiting factors
2. The temperature in the tundra is freezing.
3. Answers should include that kangaroo rats need seeds for water, so the availability of seeds is a limiting factor.
4. Answers may vary, but should include: limiting factors change from ecosystem to ecosystem and among organisms. Each crab is adapted to the conditions and food in its environment and could not survive in the other crabs' environments.

Learning Coach Guide
Lesson 6: Unit Review and Assessment

Complete this unit of study by visiting a desert ecosystem. Use all you know about organisms in ecosystems to describe food chains, food webs, limiting factors, and how organisms survive in an ecosystem that is constantly changing. If you cannot get to a desert ecosystem, go to a local ecosystem and work on the same activities.

Lesson Objectives

- Recognize that cycles in nature provide organisms with the food, air, and water they need to live, grow, and reproduce.
- Recognize that conditions within an ecosystem are constantly changing, causing plants and animals to adapt, move, or die.
- Explain that ecosystems are characterized by both their living and nonliving parts.
- Explain that certain organisms, such as insects, fungi, and bacteria, depend on dead plants and animals for food.
- Recognize examples of populations, communities, and ecosystems.
- Explain that an environment is the living and nonliving parts of an ecosystem.
- State that sunlight is the major source of energy for ecosystems, and describe how its energy is passed from organism to organism in food webs.
- Describe some ways in which organisms are dependent on each other for survival, including the need for food, pollination, and seed dispersal.
- Recognize that all organisms need some source of energy to stay alive.
- Explain how producers and consumers (herbivores, carnivores, omnivores, and decomposers) are related in food chains and food webs in an ecosystem.
- Explain that, in all environments, organisms are constantly growing, reproducing, dying, and decaying.
- Recognize that conditions within an ecosystem are constantly changing. Further recognize that some plants and animals survive because they either adapt to such changes or move to another locations, while others die.
- Recognize that objects with the same electrical charges repel and objects with different electrical charges attract.

PREPARE

Approximate lesson time is 60 minutes.

Materials

For the Student
- 📖 Ecosystems Vocabulary Review
- pencil
- 📖 Desert Ecosystem

For the Adult
- 📖 Ecosystems Vocabulary Review Answer Key
- 📖 Desert Ecosystem Answer Key

Keywords and Pronunciation

carnivore (KAHR-nuh-vor) : An animal that feeds mainly on other animals. A tiger is considered a carnivore since its diet is mainly other animals.

community : All the populations that live and interact with each other in a particular area. Frogs, ducks, insects, and fish are some of the living things that help make up a pond community.

consumer : An organism that depends on other organisms for food. Consumers directly or indirectly depend on producers for their energy. A robin is a consumer that eats worms.

decomposer : An organism that gets its energy by breaking down and consuming things that were once living, such as dead leaves, fallen branches, animal droppings, and the remains of animals and plants. Mold growing on a rotting tomato is a decomposer.

ecology : The study of the relationship between living things and their environment. A scientist studying a deer´s diet and shelter is studying ecology.

ecosystem (EE-koh-sis-tuhm) : A community of organisms interacting with one another and with their environment. Ecosystems can be large cities, vast jungles and forests, small tide pools, or even a terrarium.

food web : A diagram that combines food chains to show the interconnected feeding relationships in an ecosystem. Plants and animals can be part of more than one food chain in a food web.

herbivore (UR-buh-vor) : An animal that feeds mainly on plants. A cow is considered an herbivore since its diet is mainly plants.

limiting factor : An environmental condition that affects or limits the ability of an organism to survive. A limiting factor for an earthworm is the amount of water present in the ground.

omnivore (AHM-nih-vor) : An animal that eats both plants and animals. Bears are omnivores, and eat fruits, nuts, fish, and small animals.

photosynthesis (foh-toh-SINT-thuh-suhs)

population : A group of individuals of the same type that live in a certain area at a certain time. The population of deer grew larger every year after the wolves left the area.

producers : Organisms, such as plants or algae, that make (or produce) their own food. Plants produce their own food through the process of photosynthesis.

TEACH
Activity 1: Ecosystems: Interdependence of Life Unit Review (Online)
Instructions

Your student will review some of the key concepts presented in this unit along with some of the illustrations and photos used in the lessons. Have him read through the Explore on his own. Reinforce and explain difficult concepts as needed.

After this activity, check to see if your student can:

- Explain that ecosystems are characterized by both their living and nonliving parts.
- Explain that the physical environment is the nonliving part of an ecosystem.
- Describe some ways in which organisms are dependent on each other for survival, including the need for food, pollination, and seed dispersal.
- Recognize that all organisms need some source of energy to stay alive.
- Explain that, in all environments, organisms are constantly growing, reproducing, dying, and decaying.
- Explain that certain organisms, such as insects, fungi, and bacteria, depend on dead plants and animals for food.

- State that sunlight is the major source of energy for ecosystems, and describe how its energy is passed from organism to organism in food webs.
- Explain how producers and consumers (herbivores, carnivores, omnivores, and decomposers) are related in food chains and food webs in an ecosystem.
- Recognize that cycles in nature provide organisms with the food, air, and water they need.
- Recognize that conditions within an ecosystem are constantly changing. Further recognize that some plants and animals survive because they either adapt to such changes or move to another location, while others die.

If your student has difficulty with any of these concepts, you may wish to review the Explore with him and have him explain the key points on each screen.

Activity 2: Ecosystems Vocabulary Review (Offline)
Instructions
Your student will review the many keywords presented in this unit. Learning the vocabulary will help him make connections between the many complex relationships found among living and nonliving organisms in an ecosystem.

If your student is having difficulty with any keywords, provide him with some examples discussed in the lessons or found around your home. Then ask him to give some examples of his own.

Activity 3: Ecosystem Challenge (Offline)
Instructions
All that your student has learned about ecosystems will be put to use in this activity. He will use an illustration of a desert ecosystem and brief descriptions of the organisms that live there to answer several questions. He will be asked to create a food chain and an energy pyramid, as well as to identify herbivores and omnivores. Your student will also be asked to illustrate the carbon cycle on the illustration. If he is having difficulty remembering it, have him look back at the illustration in the Explore section.

ASSESS
Unit Assessment: Ecosystems: Interdependence of Life (Online)
Students will complete an offline Unit Assessment. Print the assessment and have students complete it on their own. Use the answer key to score the assessment, and then enter the results online. The attached answer key is the most current and may not coincide with previously printed guides.

Name _____   Date _____

Ecosystems Vocabulary Review   ANSWER KEY

Use the words in the Word Bank to fill in the blanks below.

Word Bank

herbivore	carnivore	omnivores
climate	energy pyramid	ecology
organic	inorganic	environment

1. An __**energy pyramid**__ is a diagram that shows the amount of energy present at each level of a food chain.

2. The study of living things in their environment is called __**ecology**__.

3. Matter that comes from an animal or plant and contains carbon is __**organic**__. Matter that does not come from an animal or plant such as rocks and water is __**inorganic**__.

4. A __**carnivore**__ eats only meat, while an __**herbivore**__ eats only plants. __**Omnivores**__ eat both meat and plants.

5. The usual pattern of weather an area has over a long period of time is its __**climate**__.

6. The nonliving and living things that affect an organism are part of its __**environment**__.

Ecosystems Vocabulary Review

Write the name of each level on the line next to the illustration.

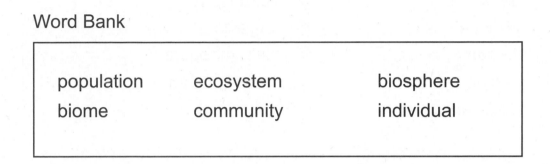

Word Bank

population	ecosystem	biosphere
biome	community	individual

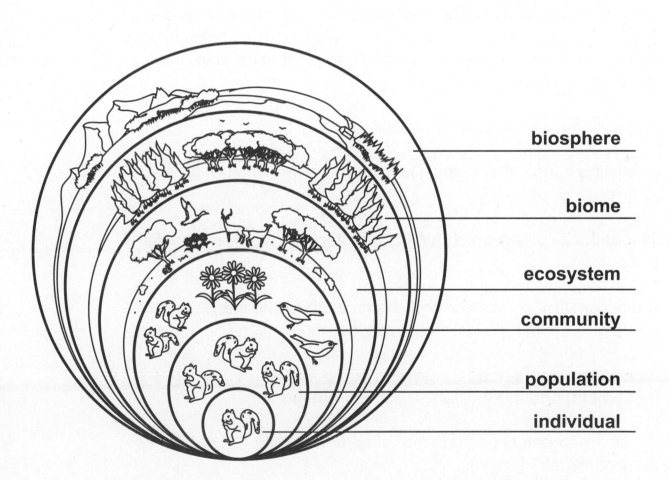

biosphere

biome

ecosystem

community

population

individual

Ecosystems Vocabulary Review

Write the letter of the matching definition on the line next to each word.

___F___ food chain   ___G___ food web

___A___ producers   ___E___ organism

___B___ consumers   ___C___ decomposers

___H___ energy   ___I___ limiting factor

___D___ scavengers

A. Organisms, such as plants or algae, that make their own food.

B. Organisms that depend on other organisms for food.

C. Organisms, such as bacteria or fungi, that get their energy by breaking down things that were once living, such as fallen leaves, dead wood, animal droppings, and dead plants and animals, causing them to decay and rot.

D. Animals that eat dead animal bodies.

E. Any living thing—that is any life form that takes in food, grows, and reproduces.

F. The pathway along which food is transferred from one organism to another.

G. A diagram that combines food chains to show the interconnected feeding relationships in an ecosystem.

H. The power plants need for growth, and animals need for growth, movement, and more. Plants get this from the sun.

I. An environmental condition that affects—or limits—the ability of an organism to survive.

Name

Date

Desert Ecosystem

Desert Ecosystem

Ecologist's Notebook

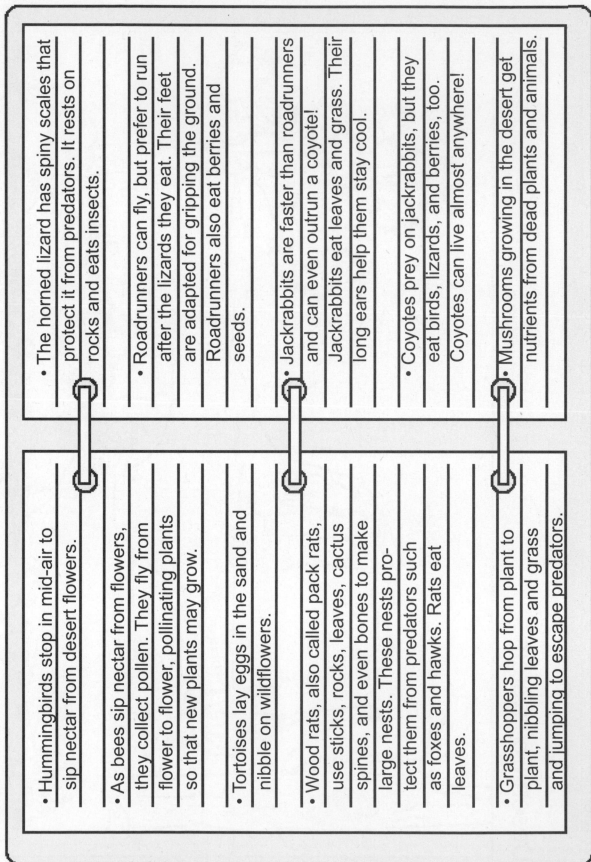

- The horned lizard has spiny scales that protect it from predators. It rests on rocks and eats insects.

- Roadrunners can fly, but prefer to run after the lizards they eat. Their feet are adapted for gripping the ground. Roadrunners also eat berries and seeds.

- Jackrabbits are faster than roadrunners and can even outrun a coyote! Jackrabbits eat leaves and grass. Their long ears help them stay cool.

- Coyotes prey on jackrabbits, but they eat birds, lizards, and berries, too. Coyotes can live almost anywhere!

- Mushrooms growing in the desert get nutrients from dead plants and animals.

- Hummingbirds stop in mid-air to sip nectar from desert flowers.

- As bees sip nectar from flowers, they collect pollen. They fly from flower to flower, pollinating plants so that new plants may grow.

- Tortoises lay eggs in the sand and nibble on wildflowers.

- Wood rats, also called pack rats, use sticks, rocks, leaves, cactus spines, and even bones to make large nests. These nests protect them from predators such as foxes and hawks. Rats eat leaves.

- Grasshoppers hop from plant to plant, nibbling leaves and grass and jumping to escape predators.

Desert Ecosystem

An ecologist studies living things in their environment. Study the animals in the Desert Ecosystem picture and read over the notes from the Ecologist's Notebook. Let's see what kind of information you can learn from studying this environment.

1. Name an herbivore and omnivore you observe in this part of the desert. Use the Ecologist's Notebook to help you. **Herbivores: hummingbird, bees, tortoise, grasshopper, jackrabbit, wood rat. Omnivores: roadrunner, coyote**

2. Create a food chain with one producer, two consumers, and a decomposer.
   Example 1: bluegrass, grasshopper, lizard, mushrooms
   Example 2: bluegrass, jackrabbit, coyote, mold

3. Draw an energy pyramid with four levels. Write the names of four desert organisms in the levels to show how energy flows through this ecosystem. The top level should be a consumer.

Desert Ecosystem

4. Describe how one organism is adapted to the environment of the desert.
Rabbits have large ears to survive in hot temperatures. Roadrunners
have feet adapted for running on the sand.

5. Do you notice a food, water, or shelter resource for which many organisms
might compete? Describe the resource and the competition. _____
Many organisms compete for producers such as wildflowers and other
plant life. These organisms are the tortoise, hummingbird, bees, and
grasshoppers.

6. Tell how the wood rat interacts with the nonliving parts of the desert.
The wood rat uses fallen sticks, leaves, rocks, and even bones to
create its nest.

7. Draw arrows on the desert illustration to show how carbon could cycle
through the desert. You may need to look back at the work you have done
with nutrient cycles in this unit.

Plants such as the cactus use carbon during photosynthesis to make
food. Herbivores such as the bee consume carbon as they eat plant
nectar. A lizard receives carbon when it eats insects such as the
bee. The roadrunner gets carbon when it eats the lizard. When the
organisms die, the mushrooms decompose them and return carbon to
the soil, to be used by plants.

Unit Assessment Answer Key

Ecosystems: Interdependence of Life

Answers:

1. flowers
2. grasshopper, frog, snake, and hawk
3. sun - flowers - grasshopper - frog - snake – hawk
4. Answers may very but should include that all living things decompose when they die.
5. algae, caterpillars, trees, and other sloths
6. muddy ground, warm climate, rain, clouds, lightning, thunder
7. Answers may vary but could include: algae depend on the sloth's fur. The caterpillar also depends on the sloth because it eats the algae growing on the sloth. The sloth depends on the trees for food and shelter.
8. a group of tree monkeys
9. a group of tree monkeys, a cluster of trees, a pile of rocks, and a fierce wind
10. a group of tree monkeys and a cluster of trees
11. sun
12. Rivers and lakes would dry up, plants could not make food and would die, animals would starve without plants to eat or would die from lack of water.
13. energy
14. all of the above
15. The desert is very hot.
16. light

Learning Coach Guide
Lesson 1: Populations

Ecologists seek to understand the relationship between individuals and their environment. They hope to clarify the relationship of an individual to its population, its competitors, its predators, its prey, and to all living things. In this unit your student will examine these relationships to get a broader view of the seemingly endless web of life that encompasses every organism on Earth.

A school of fish, a herd of cows, and a stand of maple trees--what do they have in common? All are groups of individuals of the same type that live together, or a *population.* Explore how members of a population are distributed within the area in which they live, and identify how the size of a population may change over time.

Lesson Objectives

- State that a *population* is a group of individuals of the same type living in a certain area.
- Identify individuals in a population as clumped, uniformly spaced, or randomly spaced.
- Identify birth and immigration as the two main factors that cause an increase in a population.
- Identify death and emigration as the two main factors that cause a decrease in a population.
- Calculate a change in population size.
- Define *sampling* as a way to estimate the size and distribution of a population.
- Identify the resource, such as food, sunlight, water, and space, for which organisms are competing.

PREPARE

Approximate lesson time is 60 minutes.

Materials

For the Student

    🖥 Sample the Space

    household item - shoe box lid

    pencil

    rice, uncooked

    ruler

    scissors

    🖥 Sample Your Own Space

    field guide

    sticks (4)

    magnifying glass

    paper, 8 1/2" x 11"

    string

Lesson Notes

Two quick definitions begin this lesson:

- A *population* is a group of individuals of the same species all living in one area. A species may be defined, loosely, as all individuals capable of interbreeding.
- All the different interacting populations--from oaks to robins to bacteria--form a *community*.

A *population boundary* is the edge of a particular population. It's where one population ends and another begins. In discrete situations such as termite mounds and wasp nests, it's easy to see where the population boundary is. Other times, such as in a forest, the boundary isn't so clear. Your explorer needn't feel bothered by this. Even ecologists sometimes debate where the population boundary is, and it may be more or less a distinction of convenience.

- The term *population density* means the number of individuals per unit area.

One can imaginatively think of blocking out a grassy meadow into one-yard squares and then looking to see how many beetles are in each square. Of course, even if you did this, there would not be the same number of beetles in each square, but you could still get an idea of how beetles were spaced if you gathered enough data.

There are three patterns that ecologists recognize in the spacing of individuals:

- clumped
- uniform
- random

In the *clumped* pattern, individuals group together in patches, such as deer do near the best edible plants. *Uniform* spacing means the individuals are evenly distributed, and *random* spacing means that nothing regular is influencing the placement of individuals, so they do not show any overall pattern at all.

Populations increase in two main ways:

- New individuals are born.
- Individuals *immigrate*, or enter the community from outside.

Populations decrease two main ways as well:

- Individuals die.
- Individuals *emigrate*, or leave the population.

The study of population growth and decline is critical in the preservation of endangered species, where the very survival of the species is in question.

Keywords and Pronunciation

emigration : Movement or migration out of a population. The ducks left the area when the lake dried up, and they emigrated to a lake in the next county.

immigration : Movement or migration into a population. Foxes immigrated into the national park and stayed there among the resident foxes.

migration : A regular movement of animals to a different location because of weather conditions, or of food, water, or shelter requirements. Many birds in northern lands migrate south in the winter to escape the cold weather.

population : A group of individuals of the same type that live in a certain area at a certain time. The population of deer grew larger every year after the wolves left the area.

sampling : The process of observing or counting a small part of a population as an indicator of the whole. Scientists may take a sampling of organisms to study its distribution.

TEACH
Activity 1: Changing Populations *(Online)*
Instructions
Have your student read through the Explore on her own. Reinforce and explain difficult concepts as needed.
After this activity, check to see if your student can:
- State that a *population* is a group of individuals of the same type that all live in a certain area.
- Identify individuals in a population as clumped, uniformly spaced, or randomly spaced.
- Identify birth and immigration as the two main factors that cause an increase in a population.
- Identify death and emigration as the two main factors that cause a decrease in a population.
- Calculate the change in population size.

If your student has difficulty with any of these concepts, you may wish to review the Explore with her and have her explain the key points on each screen.

Activity 2: Sample the Space *(Offline)*
Instructions
Your student will practice the sampling method used by scientists to learn about population size and distribution. She will draw a grid inside a shoebox and sprinkle a population of rice across it. She will then count the number of grains of rice within one of the squares to use as a sample of the entire population. Through additional samplings, your student will be able to observe how close the initial sampling was in estimating the size of the entire rice population.

Your student may need help drawing the grid on the bottom of the shoebox and performing the calculations.

ASSESS
Lesson Assessment: Populations (*Offline*)
Students will complete an offline assessment based on the lesson objectives. Print the assessment and have students complete it on their own. Use the answer key to score the assessment, and then enter the results online. The attached answer key is the most current and may not coincide with previously printed guides.

TEACH
Activity 3. Optional: Sample Your Own Space *(Offline)*
Instructions
Your student will learn a lot about her environment when she creates a sample plot. She will section off a square of a nearby grassy area, then take notes and make sketches of what she finds there.

Name _____ Date _____

Assessment Answer Key

1. Which of the following is a population—a spider and the fly it is about to eat or all of the oak trees in a forest?_____
   _____all of the oak trees that live in a forest_____

2. What method would a scientist use to learn about the number of individuals of a field of strawberry plants? _____
   _____sampling_____

3. Populations change from birth, death, immigration, and emigration. Which ones would cause a population to decrease? _____
   _____death or emigration_____

Look at the graphs of the number of snowy owls in two different areas of North America. Use the graphs to answer questions 4 and 5.

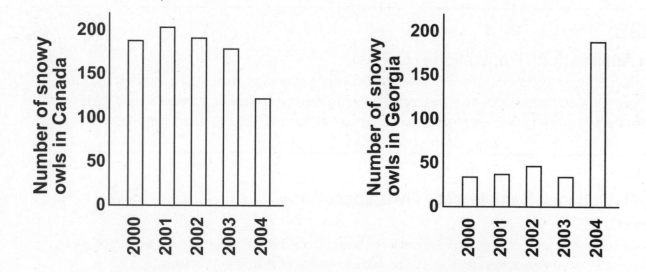

4. The snowy owl lives in the tundra, a cold biome in North America. In the year 2000, there were 200 snowy owls in a sample of the tundra. In the year 2004, there were only 126. Calculate the change in the snowy owl population size. **74** _____

Assessment Answer Key

5. Which of the following might explain the change in population of snowy owls in 2004?
    a. Snowy owls died off in Canada and Georgia
    b. Snowy owls emigrated from Canada to Georgia
    c. Snowy owls emigrated from Georgia to Canada
    d. Increased birthrates of snowy owls in Canada

6. A continuous field of bluestem prairie grass is an example of what type of population?
    a. clumped
    b. uniformly spaced
    c. randomly spaced

Learning Coach Guide
Lesson 2: Competition

How do different living things in a community use limited amounts of water, space, and food? Look at the relationships between organisms as they compete for resources within the same area.

Lesson Objectives

- Recognize ways in which organisms in a community compete for food, water, and space.
- Name two ways animals avoid, or reduce, competition (for example, moving to other habitats, eating different types of food, hunting at different times).
- Recognize that competition can occur among individuals of the same species in the same population as well as among different species in different populations.
- Identify the resource, such as food, sunlight, water, and space, for which organisms are competing.
- Recognize that in predator-prey relationships, the size of each population can change in regular cycles.

PREPARE

Approximate lesson time is 60 minutes.

Materials

For the Student
- Hare-y Competition

For the Adult
- Hare-y Competition Answer Key

Lesson Notes

Changing environmental conditions are one of the causes of changes in populations. When there are either more or fewer animals in a herd, or plants in a meadow, than there were in the past, it is reasonable to look for factors in the environment to explain the change.

The availability of resources is often the factor that most determines how many members of a population will exist. Amounts of food, water, and living space will determine how many members of a population can survive.

- Because these factors limit the ability of organisms to survive, they are known as *limiting factors*.

Living things compete for limited resources. This is inevitable. The world itself can sustain only a finite number of living things. The same is true of any smaller section of the world--say, a grassy meadow where a population of crickets lives. Competition for resources happens in two ways:

- Competition can occur between members of the same species, in the same population.
- Competition can occur between members of different species, in different populations.

When locusts swarm over fields and eat up all the grain, they are in competition with other grain-eating animals for a limited food supply. Even within the swarm, however, the faster and stronger locusts may be getting more food than the slower or weaker ones. There is competition within the species and competition between species.

Living space is another type of limiting factor. Every living thing needs space in which to find food, reproduce, and grow. Planting a thousand seeds in a tiny garden patch won't produce a thousand flowers: most will be crowded out and not survive because the limited space cannot accommodate them all.

Organisms find various ways of reducing the pressure of competition to increase their own chances of survival. These include:

- Moving. Animals that can move may simply travel to a new location to avoid over-population problems.
- Feeding on different foods. If a species eats a kind of food that is not eaten by a second species, the two will not have to compete.
- Feeding at different times. An organism, such as an owl, may feed on the same thing as another organism, such as a hawk. But the owl feeds at night and a hawk feeds during the day.,
- Defending territory. Territorial animals, such as wolves, many fish, and even songbirds will defend particular areas where there are good resources.

The result of competition is that the organisms become better adapted to their environments and will be more likely to reproduce in that environment than the ones that aren't as well adapted.

Keywords and Pronunciation

competition : The struggle between two or more organisms or two or more kinds of organisms for resources in short supply. Lions in the same population are in competition with each other for food resources.

Galápagos (guh-LAH-puh-guhs)

resource : Materials from the environment that living things use to live and grow. Food, water, and shelter are resources animals need to survive.

TEACH
Activity 1: Competition (Online)
Instructions
Have your student read through the Explore on her own. Reinforce and explain difficult concepts as needed.

Explore Suggestions:
Before you begin, think about the resources for animals and plants that live in your area--in a park or backyard near you. What sorts of resources may be in limited supply there? As practice, ask too what are the limited resources for the people in your town. Consider water, temperature, and other factors.

After this activity, check to see if your student can:
- Recognize ways that organisms in a community compete for food, water, and space.
- Name two ways animals avoid or reduce competition, such as moving to other habitats, eating different types of food, and hunting at different times.
- Recognize that competition can occur among individuals of the same species in the same population and among different species in different populations.
- Identify the resource, such as food, sunlight, water, and space, for which organisms are competing.

If your student has difficulty with any of these concepts, you may wish to review the Explore with her and have her explain the key points on each screen.

Activity 2: Hare-y Competition *(Online)*
Instructions

Your student will use an interactive simulation to observe a population of hares competing for limited resources. In each round of the game, she will choose which limited resource--food, water or shelter--each hare will seek.

If the hare finds the resources it needs, it will live another year and reproduce, creating another hare for the next round. If the hare cannot find the resource it needs, it will die of starvation, dehydration, or lack of shelter. Eventually, it will decompose and become part of the environment again.

Your student will chart how many hares she has after each year, and create a bar graph with her data.

At the end of this activity, check to see if your student can:
- Recognize ways that organisms in a community compete for food, water, and space.
- Recognize that competition can occur among individuals of the same species in the same population as well as among different species in different populations.
- Identify the resource, such as food, sunlight, water, and space, for which organisms are competing.

ASSESS

Lesson Assessment: Competition (*Online*)

Students will complete an offline assessment based on the lesson objectives. Print the assessment and have students complete it on their own. Use the answer key to score the assessment, and then enter the results online. The attached answer key is the most current and may not coincide with previously printed guides.

Hare-y Competition Answer Key

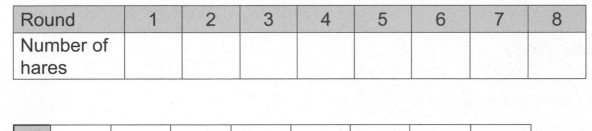

Round	1	2	3	4	5	6	7	8
Number of hares								

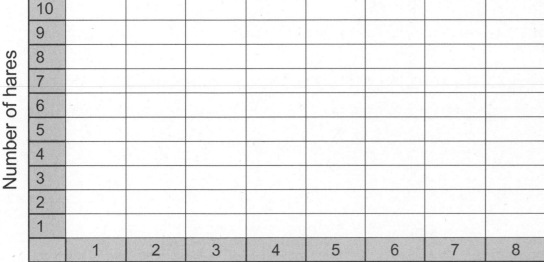

Number of hares / Years

What do you notice about the hare population? _____
        The population increases and decreases.

_____

How can you tell when competition among hares was greatest?
What happened next? _____
        When there are little resources and a lot of hares.
        The next year, a lot of hares die.

_____

If you continued to play 10 or 20 more rounds, do you think you
would get a different population graph? Why or why not?
        No, the population would continue to rise and
        fall. Or, it would die out completely from lack of
        the needed resources.

Lesson Assessment Answer Key

Competition

1. food, water, and space or shelter

2. different species

3. Answers may vary but should include their beaks are different sizes and shapes so they eat different types of seeds.

4. Answers may vary but should include they hunt at different times so they never compete for their prey at the same time.

5. sunlight

Learning Coach Guide
Lesson 3: Predators and Prey

Explore the relationships between predator and prey populations by seeing both how organisms eat and how they avoid being eaten. Learn about various adaptations organisms have developed that let them locate and capture prey, and how the prey have adapted to defending themselves. Learn how predator-prey relationships can affect population sizes.

Lesson Objectives

- Recognize that predator-prey relationships can help balance the structure of the community.
- Identify ways predators locate and capture their prey.
- Identify ways prey defend themselves against predators.
- Recognize that in predator-prey relationships, the size of each population can change in regular cycles.

PREPARE

Approximate lesson time is 60 minutes.

Materials

For the Student

    📖 The Graph Tells It All

    pencil

For the Adult

    📖 The Graph Tells It All Answer Key

Lesson Notes

In this lesson your student will begin to study some things about the interactions of populations in an ecosystem. Keep in mind that while populations change size due to environmental changes, the adaptations that organisms have play an essential role as well.

In any ecosystem there is a struggle for life. Animals eat plants, microorganisms feed on animals, and viruses destroy bacteria. Different populations fight for water, nesting sites, or food. Among the most dramatic of these interactions is the predator-prey struggle. Though your student may cringe at the site of a rabbit being hunted down by a fox, this is part of the great drama of life. In fact, such interactions balance an ecosystem, keeping the number of both predator and prey within prescribed limits. Any upset in these natural predator-prey cycles can send certain population numbers sky-high while reducing others to near extinction.

Over time, scientists find predators have become adapted to their roles in ways we find striking. The fangs of a snake, the speed of a cheetah, and the sting of scorpion are all adaptations for predation. Herbivores are like predators. The teeth of deer or the tongue of a giraffe are also adaptations--for preying on plants. But just as predators have evolved amazing mechanisms to get food, so prey have evolved in response. The skunk warns us not to come near. You need to encounter a stinging nettle only once to avoid it the next time. In fact, many scientists view much of nature in terms of adaptations that an organism has developed to survive encounters with other organisms.

So in any ecosystem nature comes to a balance. As time goes by this balance may shift: one population rises and another falls. This is the natural way; populations are always in flux. People can also move the balance of many populations by our activities. Your student will see one example on the last few screens of this lesson. In short: humans now eat a lot of fish from an area; seals in the area have fewer fish to eat, so there are fewer seals. This means killer whales have fewer seals to eat, so they eat otters instead. Otters eat sea urchins; fewer otters means more sea urchins. Since urchins eat kelp, more sea urchins means smaller kelp forests. The lesson is the same as in the first few screens: There is a complex balance in nature, and we are a part of that balance.

Keywords and Pronunciation

herbivore (UR-buh-vor) : An animal that feeds mainly on plants. A cow is considered an herbivore since its diet is mainly plants.

predator : An animal that hunts for food. A hawk is a predator of mice.

prey : An animal or plant that is hunted for food. Berries and birds are both prey for the desert coyote.

TEACH
Activity 1: Predators and Prey (Online)
Instructions
Have your student read through the Explore on her own. Reinforce and explain difficult concepts as needed.

Explore Suggestions:
Screen 6: Have your student research the Dungeness crab to find out what nonliving and living factors contribute to the changes in its population.
After this activity, check to see if your student can:
- Identify ways predators locate and capture their prey.
- Identify ways prey defend themselves against predators.
- Recognize that predator-prey relationships can help balance the structure of the community.
- Recognize that in predator-prey relationships, the size of each population can change in regular cycles.

If your student has difficulty with any of these concepts, you may wish to review the Explore with her and have her explain the key points on each screen.

Activity 2: The Graph Tells It All (Offline)
Instructions
Scientists use graphs to show the rise and fall of population size over time. Your student will study some graphs to learn about predator-prey relationships that affect population sizes. She will interpret the information from the graphs to draw conclusions about what is causing the rise and fall in each scenario. She will also use information from a chart to create her own bar graph for a population of lemmings and arctic foxes.

ASSESS

Lesson Assessment: Predators and Prey (Online)
Students will complete an offline assessment based on the lesson objectives. Print the assessment and have students complete it on their own. Use the answer key to score the assessment, and then enter the results online. The attached answer key is the most current and may not coincide with previously printed guides.

Name _____   Date _____

The Graph Tells It All Answer Key

Population Graphs
Graphs can show changes in population.

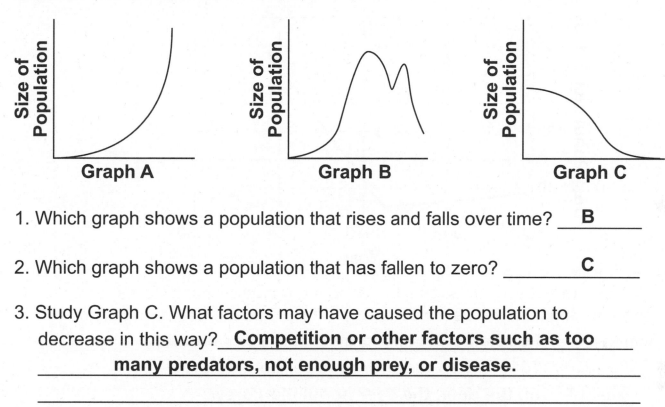

1. Which graph shows a population that rises and falls over time? __**B**__

2. Which graph shows a population that has fallen to zero? _____**C**_____

3. Study Graph C. What factors may have caused the population to
   decrease in this way? __**Competition or other factors such as too**__
   _____**many predators, not enough prey, or disease.**_____

   _____

The Graph Tells It All Answer Key

Deer Population Changes

This graph shows changes in a population of deer in Arizona between 1890 and 1930. These deer lived in a canyon along with mountain lions, which prey on deer. Notice how the deer population rises and falls.

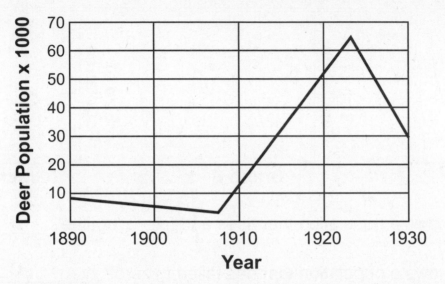

1. Can you tell what year people began killing mountain lions? Look for a sharp increase in the deer population. Why would the deer population increase? **People began killing mountain lions around 1910. When there were fewer lions to prey on the deer, the deer population grew.**

2. Find where the deer population was highest. With so many deer competing for resources, what happened next? **The deer population decreased, maybe from lack of food, water, or shelter.**

The Graph Tells It All Answer Key

The Lynx and the Hare

You can use graphs to study more than one population at a time. For example, about every 7 years, the snowshoe hare population rises, then crashes. Canada lynx population does the same thing, a year behind the hares. Look at this graph of the lynx and hare population.

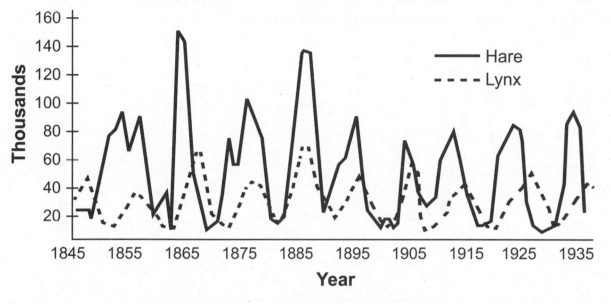

1. What happens after the hare population falls? _____
   The lynx population falls a year later.

2. Which is the predator, the lynx or the hare? **the lynx**

3. How do you know which organisms are the predators and which are the prey? **The population of lynx crashes right after the population of hares does. Fewer hares means less food for the lynx, so the lynx population decreases. As the hare population starts to rise, the lynx population rises, because there is more food available in the form of prey.**

The Graph Tells It All Answer Key

The Wolf and the Moose
The wolf is a predator of the moose. A moose is very strong, so wolves usually will attack only moose that are old, sick, or young. At one time, a small herd of Canadian moose walked across a frozen lake to Isle Royale, an island in North America. There was a large supply of food for the moose. Soon, wolves reached the same island. This graph shows the changes in the wolf and moose population on the island.

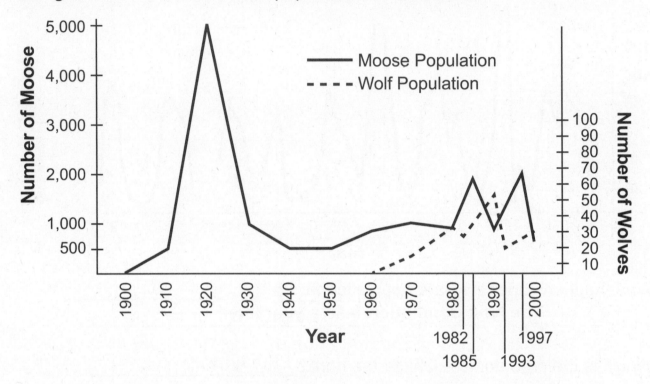

1. During what year was the moose population largest?____**1920**____

2. By 1928, the moose had eaten most of the plants they liked to eat. What happened next? ____**The moose population**____ ____**crashed due to lack of resources.**____

3. Study the wolf population. In 1980, many wolves became sick with a virus. What happened to the moose population? __**The moose**__ __**population grew because there were not as many wolf predators.**__

4. What happened when the moose population grew too large again? ____**It decreased from competition for resources.**____

The Graph Tells It All Answer Key

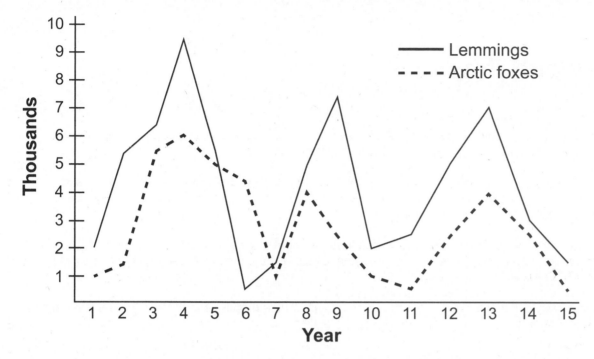

1. Which is the predator and which is the prey?__**The arctic fox is the**__
   __**predator and the lemming is the prey.**__

2. How can you tell from the graph? ___**The fox population rises after**___
   __**the lemming population rises, then crashes after the lemming**__
   __**population crashes. A high population of lemmings provides**__
   __**more prey for the fox. When the population of lemmings**__
   __**decreases, there is less food for the fox.**__

Lesson Assessment Answer Key

Predators and Prey

1. Answers may vary but could include: predators may use their sense such as sight and smell to locate prey. They may use claws, fangs, stingers, or poison to capture prey.

2. Answers may vary but could include: they may run, hide, make alarm calls, use camouflage, or spray a chemical. Plants may have thorns or thick waxy leaves that are tough to chew. Plants may also have chemicals that are poisonous to predators.

3. Answers may vary but could include: a decrease in the amount of prey available for the arctic fox causes the fox population to fall. When the population of the fox's prey begins to increase again, so does the population of the arctic fox.

4. Answers may vary but could include: the predators would eat the rabbits, and there would be less rabbits to destroy farm plants.

Learning Coach Guide
Lesson 4: Symbiosis

Study *symbiosis*, the interaction between two different kinds of organisms in which at least one benefits from the relationship. Distinguish among the three different types of symbiotic relationships: mutualism, commensalism, and parasitism.

Lesson Objectives

- Explain that the annual flooding of rivers allowed people to grow grain such as rice.
- Define *mutualism* as an interaction between two organisms in which both benefit from the relationship.
- Define *commensalism* as an interaction between two organisms in which one organism gains from the relationship and the neither benefits nor harms the other.
- Define *parasitism* as an interaction between two organisms in which one gains from the relationship and harms the other.
- Recognize that organisms in an ecosystem can compete for resources such as food, shelter, and water.
- Identify symbiotic relationships between organisms (mutualism, commensalism, and parasitism).

PREPARE

Approximate lesson time is 60 minutes.

Materials

> For the Student
>> 🖥 Relationship Studies
>
>> pencil
>
> For the Adult
>> 🖥 Relationship Studies Answer Key

Lesson Notes

Plants and animals in a community interact with each other in many different ways. Some live very close together in a kind of partnership called *symbiosis.* When two individuals come together and at least one of them is helped by the partnership, we say they have a *symbiotic relationship.*

There are three different types of symbiotic relationships:

- Parasitism
- Mutualism
- Commensalism

In *parasitism*, one organism benefits and the other is harmed. The parasite gets its food from the other organism, the host. The parasite benefits from feeding on the host, but the host is harmed in the process. Parasites such as tapeworms live inside their hosts. Other parasites, such as fleas, ticks, and lice, live on the host's skin. Some parasites are plants. Mistletoe is one such plant parasite.

In *mutualism*, the two organisms help each other and neither one is harmed. Butterflies and bees, for example, help flowering plants by pollinating the flowers. The plants help the insects by providing nectar for the insects to eat.

Commensalism is the third type of symbiotic relationship. Here, only one organism benefits. The other does not benefit, but it is also not harmed. When a bird builds a nest in a tree, the tree shelters the bird. The bird neither harms nor helps the tree.

In some cases, commensalism may turn into parasitism or mutualism. For example:

- Barnacles that attach to a whale do not normally harm the whale. As long as the whale can move about freely, the relationship can be called commensalism. But if the barnacles slow down the whale, they become parasites.
- An egret feeding on insects flushed out of the grass by a grazing cow is an example of commensalism. When the same egret perches on the cow's back and eats ticks and other parasites off the cow's skin, the relationship becomes mutualism.

Keywords and Pronunciation

acacia (uh-KAY-shuh)

commensalism (kuh-MEN-suh-lih-zuhm) : A symbiotic relationship in which one organism benefits and the other neither benefits nor is harmed. Barnacles attached to a whale is an example of commensalism.

mutualism (MYOO-chuh-wuh-lih-zuhm) : A symbiotic relationship in which both types of organism help each other and both benefit. Bees pollinating flowers as they sip the flowers´ nectar is an example of mutualism.

parasitism (PAIR-uh-suh-tih-zuhm) : A symbiotic relationship in which one organism benefits and the other is harmed. A leech attaching to a host´s body and sucking the host´s blood is an example of parasitism.

symbiosis (sim-biy-OH-sis) : A relationship between two organisms that interact in a way that benefits at least one of them. A tick and a dog live in symbiosis.

TEACH
Activity 1: Helpful and Harmful Relationships *(Online)*
Instructions

Have your student read through the Explore on her own. Reinforce and explain difficult concepts as needed.

After this activity, check to see if your student can:

- Identify symbiotic relationships between organisms as mutualism, commensalism, or parasitism.
- Define *mutualism* as an interaction between two organisms where both benefit from the relationship.
- Define *commensalism* as an interaction between two organisms where one gains from the relationship and the other neither benefits nor is harmed.
- Define *parasitism* as an interaction between two organisms where one gains from the relationship while harming the other.

If your student has difficulty with any of these concepts, you may wish to review the Explore with her and have her explain the key points on each screen.

Activity 2: Relationship Studies (Offline)
Instructions
Various scenarios will be provided describing symbiotic relationships among several organisms. Your student will be asked to identify whether the partnership shows mutualism, commensalism, or parasitism.

ASSESS
Lesson Assessment: Symbiosis (Online)
Students will complete an offline assessment based on the lesson objectives. Print the assessment and have students complete it on their own. Use the answer key to score the assessment, and then enter the results online. The attached answer key is the most current and may not coincide with previously printed guides.

Name _____   Date _____

Relationship Studies Answer Key

Plants and animals may have one of three types of relationships:
   Mutualism - Two organisms gain from the relationship.
Commensalism - One organism gains from the relationship and the other neither benefits nor is harmed.
   Parasitism - One organism gains from the relationship while harming the other.

Read about the organisms below and tell what kind of relationship they have.

1. Snails make shells, then leave the shells. Hermit crabs find homes inside the empty snail shells. The snail is not harmed. **commensalism**

2. A honey guide bird shows a honey badger the way to beehive. The badger breaks open the hive and eats honey. The bird also eats the honey. **mutualism**

3. Mistletoe grows on an oak tree. The oak tree loses water and nutrients to the mistletoe. **parasitism**

4. Insects stick to a buffalo's hair as it walks through the grass. A cowbird eats the insects and does not harm the buffalo. **commensalism**

5. Ticks feed on a rhinoceros' blood. **parasitism**

6. Oxpeckers eat ticks on a rhinoceros. **mutualism**

7. Yucca moths lay eggs in yucca flowers. When the eggs hatch, the larvae eat the yucca seeds. The adult moths pollinate the flowers. **mutualism**

8. Bacteria live in your intestines. They make vitamin K, which is good for your blood. They also help digest food. **mutualism**

9. A different type of bacteria enters your body when you eat bad food or water. It causes you to lose fluids your body needs. **parasitism**

10. Sea anemones have stinging tentacles. A clownfish lives among the sea anemones without being stung. The clownfish helps clean the sea anemones. **mutualism**

Lesson Assessment Answer Key

Symbiosis

1. symbiotic

2. commensalism

3. mutualism

4. mutualism

5. parasitism

Learning Coach Guide
Lesson 5: Animal Behavior

The way an organism responds to its environment is its *behavior*. Behaviors can be either innate or learned. Distinguish between these types of behaviors. Study the dynamics of animals that live and work together in groups. Observe pill bug behaviors and determine whether or not their behaviors are learned or innate.

Lesson Objectives

- Identify behaviors as innate or learned.
- State that a *population* is a group of individuals of the same type living in a certain area.
- Identify symbiotic relationships between organisms (mutualism, commensalism, and parasitism).
- Identify behaviors that help animals survive.
- Recognize that members of a society have special roles and work together to increase the group's chances of survival.
- Recognize that organisms in an ecosystem can compete for resources such as food, shelter, and water.
- Classify organisms as predators and prey.
- Describe factors that affect the growth of a population.
- Explain that living things cause changes in their ecosystems, and that some of these changes are detrimental to other organisms, and some are beneficial.
- Explain that an animal's behavior helps it survive.
- State that a population is a group of individuals of the same type living in a certain area.

PREPARE

Approximate lesson time is 60 minutes.

Advance Preparation

- If you choose to do this alternate activity, you will need at least 10 live pill bugs (isopods). You can find them living under logs, moist leaves, flowerpots, outdoor pet dishes, or under paving bricks or stones. You may also purchase them from Carolina Biological at carolina.com. Allow a couple of weeks for delivery.

Materials

For the Student

    📖 Pill Bug Behaviors

    pencil

    📖 Alternate Activity: Pill Bug Behaviors

    household item - aluminum foil

    household item - bowl (2)

    household item - dish

    household item - ice cubes

---

pill bugs

markers - black permanent

water - warm

paper, 8 1/2" x 11"

For the Adult

⊞ Pill Bug Behaviors Answer Key

Lesson Notes

The ways in which a living thing responds to its environment are known as its *behavior*. Organisms behave in response to some sort of stimulus; a *stimulus*, in turn, is anything that causes a reaction or response. Behaviors can result from either an outside or an inside stimulus. The sight of a predator is an example of an outside stimulus, while hunger pains are an inside stimulus. Often, organisms respond to a combination of both inner and outer stimuli.

Scientists have identified two main types of behavior--*innate* and *learned*. An innate behavior is one that does not have to be taught. A baby bird inside an egg, for instance, already knows how to peck its way out. Innate behaviors can be simple or complex. If you touch something hot, you jerk your hand back without thinking. Baby birds whose eyes are not yet open automatically beg for food when they feel their parents landing on the nest. Pill bugs move away from bright light. Plant stems grow toward light, while roots grow downward into the dirt. These are all simple innate behaviors.

Instincts are more complex innate behaviors. Some species of birds migrate long distances in the fall. Other animals, such as woodchucks or frogs, hibernate to survive through cold winter months. These complex actions are examples of instinctual behavior.

Learned behaviors develop as an organism goes through life, and help the organism survive changes in its environment. A predator figuring out how to hunt by watching its parents is developing a learned behavior. Reading and telling time are two human forms of learned behavior.

One form of learned behavior is called *imprinting*. Imprinting happens during a specific time in an animal's life, usually right after the animal is born. When an animal "imprints on" something, it simply responds to, and identifies with, the first object it encounters.

Scientist Konrad Lorenz discovered imprinting. Just after a group of ducklings hatched from their eggs, Lorenz stood near them and imitated the mother duck's quacking sounds. From that point on, the ducks thought of Lorenz as their mother and followed him around everywhere. Even when the ducks grew older, they preferred to be near humans instead of other ducks. The ducks had imprinted on humans.

Social behavior is another form of learned behavior. Social behavior takes place when organisms live together in groups. Many animals live in groups called *societies*.

There are many kinds of social behavior. Some animals have mating rituals. This behavior helps strengthen the bond between the male and female pairs. Animals may also compete with each other for food, territory, or mates. Male mountain goats ram heads together until the weakest goat backs down. These tests help develop a social structure within the mountain goats' community.

Some animals, such as ants and honeybees, live in groups where each member has a specific job to do. When organisms work together, the chances are greater that their community will survive.

Keywords and Pronunciation

behavior : The way in which an organism responds to its environment. Behaviors may be learned or innate.

imprinting : Developing behaviors during a specific period of time. Imprinting usually occurs right after an organism is born.

innate : A type of behavior that is "built in" or does not have to be learned. Moving away from light is an innate behavior of pill bugs.

social behavior : Any interaction between organisms of the same kind. Male mountain goats fighting to defend their territory is a social behavior.

societies : Groups in which organisms live. Bees are an example of organisms that live in societies.

stimulus (STIM-yuh-luhs) : Anything in the environment that causes a reaction or response. A hunting dog will respond to the stimulus of a nearby bird.

TEACH
Activity 1: Behaviors (Online)
Instructions
Have your student read through the Explore on her own. Reinforce and explain difficult concepts as needed.

Explore Suggestions:

Screen 4: Have your student describe two of her behaviors--one innate and one learned. Innate behaviors include blinking, stretching, sneezing, or salivating.

Screen 7: There are certain careers that deal with animal behavior. Have your student choose an animal, or person, to watch. Have her observe five different actions, then name each behavior. Have her identify the behaviors as either innate or learned.

Screen 7: Many other animals have interesting behaviors. Have your student look in books about birds, bats, insects, and primates such as baboons to find out more about unusual animal behaviors.

After this activity, check to see if your student can:

- Identify behaviors as innate or learned.
- Identify behaviors that help animals survive.
- Recognize that members of a society have special roles and work together to increase the group's chances of survival.

If your student has difficulty with any of these concepts, you may wish to review the Explore with her and have her explain the key points on each screen.

Activity 2: Pill Bug Behaviors *(Offline)*
Instructions

Teaching: Your student will study the data collected from an experiment with pill bug behavior. It is strongly recommended that you also try the experiment with pill bugs on your own. Your student should understand the difference between learned and innate behaviors. She will observe two types of pill bug behaviors, both innate, and then see whether these behaviors are necessary for survival.

What to Expect: Pill bugs survive only in cold climates, so the data in Experiment 1 reflects this fact. Pill bugs respond to touch by curling up into a ball. This behavior is necessary for survival. Discuss with your student whether or not this action may be in response to a predator. Do people respond to danger the same way?

Answers:

Experiment 1:

1. It would be found in a cold climate

2. innate

3. Pill bugs cannot survive in hot temperatures so they will move to a cooler climate.

Experiment 2:

4. Pill bugs curl into a ball when they are touched.

5. innate

6. If they are in danger of attack, they may curl up to hide or protect themselves from predators.

Activity 3. Optional: Alternate Activity: Pill Bug Behaviors *(Offline)*
Instructions

Teaching: Your student should understand the difference between learned and innate behaviors. She will observe two types of pill bug behaviors, both innate, and then determine whether or not these behaviors are necessary for survival.

What to Expect: Some species of pill bugs survive only in cold climates, and their behavior is reflected in Experiment 1. In Experiment 2, the pill bugs will respond to touch by curling up into a ball. This behavior is necessary for survival as well. Discuss with your student what this may be in response to. Do people respond to danger the same way?

Answers:

Experiment 1:

1. It would be found in a cold climate.

2. innate

3. Pill bugs cannot survive in hot temperatures, so they will move to cooler climates.

Experiment 2:

4. Pill bugs curl into a ball when they are touched.

5. innate

6. If they are in danger of attack, they may curl up to hide or protect themselves from predators.

ASSESS

Lesson Assessment: Animal Behavior (*Online*)

Students will complete an offline assessment based on the lesson objectives. Print the assessment and have students complete it on their own. Use the answer key to score the assessment, and then enter the results online. The attached answer key is the most current and may not coincide with previously printed guides.

TEACH

Activity 4. Optional: Habit Forming Behavior (*Offline*)

Instructions

Your student will experiment with changing learned behaviors. She will be asked to write her name with the opposite hand she is used to using. After two weeks of writing her name with the opposite hand, she may find it easier than she did at first.

Name _____   Date _____

Pill Bug Behaviors

Pill bugs live under logs, moist leaves, flower pots, outdoor pet dishes, bricks, and stones. They are omnivores that eat decaying plants and animals. Pill bugs breathe through gills.

EXPERIMENT 1
Ten pill bugs were placed on an aluminum foil tray. The tray was divided into three sections—A, B, and C as shown below. A bowl of warm water was placed at one end of the tray. A bowl of ice cubes was placed at the opposite end. The bugs were placed in section B.

The illustrations below show where the bugs were after 5 minutes and after 10 minutes.

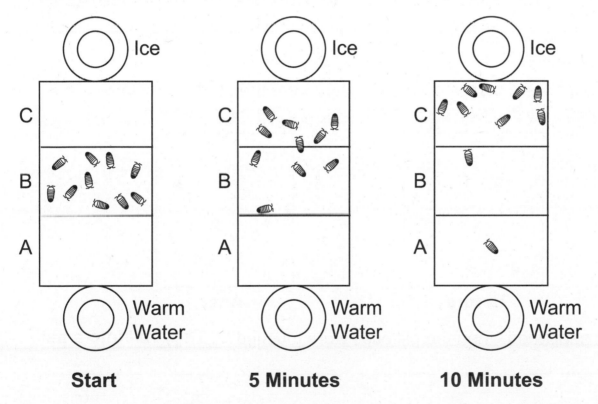

| Start | 5 Minutes | 10 Minutes |

The chart on the next page shows where the pill bugs were at the end of 10 minutes. The data below that shows two more trials of the same experiment.

Pill Bug Behaviors Answer Key

Trial	Section A	Section B	Section C
1	1	1	8
2	0	3	7
3	0	1	9

1. Based on the information gathered, in what type of climate would a pill bug probably live? __**It would be found in a cold climate.**__

2. Would you describe the pill bugs' behavior in this experiment as *innate* or *learned*? __**innate**__

3. How might this behavior help pill bugs survive? _____**Pill bugs can not**_____ __**survive in hot temperatures, so they move to cooler climates.**__

EXPERIMENT 2

Five pill bugs were placed on a dish. They were then touched gently with a pencil. Study the illustration below to see how the bugs reacted.

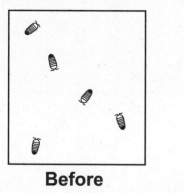
Before

After

4. What happened when the pill bugs were touched? __**They roll into a ball.**__

5. Would you describe this behavior as *innate* or *learned*? __**innate**__

6. How might this behavior help pill bugs survive? _____**If they are in**_____ __**danger of attack, they may curl up to hide or protect**__ __**themselves from predators.**__

Lesson Assessment Answer Key

Animal Behavior

1. Innate

2. Answers may vary but should include: Carp did not normally swim to the surface for food when people were nearby. They learn to do this only after people fed them a few times.

3. Ground squirrels curl up and become inactive in cold weather.
   Pill bugs curl up when they sense danger.

4. Answers may vary but should include: In a honeybee colony, all of the bees have special jobs and roles to produce more members of the colony. The queen mates and lays all the eggs, Drones mate with the queen then die soon after. Worker bees feed the bee larvae.

Learning Coach Guide
Lesson 6: Unit Review and Assessment

Your student will review what she has learned by studying some interactions taking place in a national park. She will match important words she has learned with their definitions.

Lesson Objectives

- Identify behaviors as innate or learned.
- Identify symbiotic relationships between organisms (mutualism, commensalism, and parasitism).
- State that a population is a group of individuals of the same type living in a certain area.
- Recognize that organisms in an ecosystem can compete for resources such as food, shelter, and water.
- Classify organisms as predators and prey.
- Describe factors that affect the growth of a population.
- Explain that living things cause changes in their ecosystems, and that some of these changes are detrimental to other organisms, and some are beneficial.
- Explain that an animal's behavior helps it survive.

PREPARE

Approximate lesson time is 60 minutes.

Materials

For the Student

    🖳 Vocabulary Review Concentration

      pencil

    🖳 Brewster Ridge National Park

Lesson Notes

There are many key concepts in the Plant and Animal Interactions unit. The bulleted list below highlights these key concepts that are covered in each lesson. Use the list as a guide during the activities to help your student review before taking the Unit Assessment.

- A *population* is a group of individuals of the same type all living in a particular area.
- Spacing patterns of individuals within a population can vary greatly due to differences in environmental conditions.
- The overall size of a population can change over time. Populations increase when organisms join a population through birth or immigration. Populations decrease as organisms leave it through death or emigration.
- When two or more populations share the same resources, they compete for those resources. Competition can occur among individuals of the same species in the same population or between different species in different populations.

- Predators also have adaptations such as claws, fangs, stingers, or poison. Predators that chase their prey are usually fast and agile. Other predators are camouflaged and wait to ambush their prey when they get close enough.
- Prey defenses include running, hiding, and fighting. Some sound alarm calls to alert others of intruders while others use camouflage to make it difficult for attacker to spot them.
- Plants cannot run or hide, so they produce chemical poisons, spines, thorns, thick waxy leaves, or hairs that make it difficult for insects to travel through them. Some even release sticky liquids that trap insects.
- Predator-prey relationships help maintain balance in an ecosystem.
- Organisms may interact in very close associations, often even living in direct contact with each other. Two different kinds of organism living together in a close relationship that benefits at least one of them is called *symbiosis*.
- There are three different types of symbiotic relationships: mutualism, parasitism, and commensalism. These relationships are classified according to how each pair of organisms interacts.
- The way in which an organism responds to its environment is known as its *behavior*. Behaviors occur as a result of some type of stimulus. A *stimulus* is anything that causes a reaction or response. Scientists identify two main types of behavior: innate and learned.
- Learned behaviors are a result of an animal's experience and acquired after birth.
- Many other organisms exhibit complex social behavior as they compete for territory, food, or mates. Insects, such as honeybees, termites, and ants form complex social colonies in which each individual has a specific function.

TEACH
Activity 1: Vocabulary Review Concentration *(Offline)*
Instructions
Play Vocabulary Concentration with your student to help her review the words learned in this unit. Pay special attention to difficult concepts, such as the difference between immigration and emigration and the differences between the three types of symbiotic relationships.

Answers:

sampling: The process of observing or counting a small part of a population as an indicator of the whole.

migration: A regular, usually long-distance, movement of animals to a different location.

immigration: Movement or migration into a population.

emigration: Movement or migration out of a population.

competition: The struggle between two or more organisms or two or more kinds of organisms for resources in short supply.

predator: An animal that hunts for food.

prey: An animal or plant that is hunted for food.

symbiosis: A relationship between two different kinds of organisms that live together in a way that benefits at least one of them.

mutualism: A symbiotic relationship in which both types of organisms help each other and both benefit.

parasitism: A symbiotic relationship in which one organism benefits and the other is harmed.

commensalism: A symbiotic relationship in which one organism benefits and the other neither benefits nor is harmed.

behavior: The way in which an organism responds to its environment.

stimulus: Anything in the environment that causes a reaction or response.

innate: A type of behavior that is "built in" or does not have to be learned.

imprinting: Developing behaviors during a specific period of time.

social behavior: Any interaction between organisms of the same kind.

Activity 2: Brewster Ridge National Park (Offline)
Instructions

Your student will review the concepts presented in this unit as they relate to the unit objectives. She will answer questions about interactions in a fictitious national park. You may wish to read the information with her. Have her check earlier lesson notes and activities to help her complete the activity.

Your student should have a good understanding of the interactions that take place in this fictional national park. She should be able to understand population changes, describe symbiotic relationships, and understand predator-prey relationships.

Answers:

Bison and Brucellosis- A Dangerous Relationship

1. bison

2. Study the population graph.

A. The 1800s.

B. In the 1900s.

C. The population decreased. It is emigration.

D. The population grew. In 1996 bison had to compete for resources during a harsh winter. The population decreased.

3. parasitism

Lake Trout

4. lake trout, cutthroat trout, pelicans, otters, black bears, minks, ospreys, loons, bald eagles, and grizzly bears

5. a bad change because it decreased the food resources for other animals

6. lake trout, pelicans, otters, black bears, minks, ospreys, loons, bald eagles, and grizzly bears.

7. They are competing for food. If there is not enough food, the populations will decrease as organisms die.

8. No, lake trout are impossible to catch because they live in deep water.

Black Bears at Brewster Ridge

9. Choosing a den, dropping body temperature, slowing breathing, hibernating, eating food from humans, begging, grunting at danger

10. Innate: Choosing a den, dropping body temperature, slowing breathing, hibernating, grunting at danger. Learned: eating food from humans, begging

ASSESS

Unit Assessment: Plant and Animal Interactions (*Online*)

Students will complete an offline Unit Assessment. Print the assessment and have students complete it on their own. Use the answer key to score the assessment, and then enter the results online. The attached answer key is the most current and may not coincide with previously printed guides.

Name _____   Date _____

Unit Assessment Answer Key

Plant and Animal Interactions

1. Answers may vary but should include a group of individuals of the same type that live in a certain area.

2. food, water, and shelter or space

3. Answers may vary but could include: Zebra will have to compete with other zebras and other kinds of animals for water to drink. Less water means that other organisms that zebra eat will not be available for food. Also, less water will affect trees that provide shelter for the zebra. There will not be as much available shelter.

4. Increase: birth and immigration
   Decrease: death and emigration

5. It decreased the cutthroat trout population.

6. Predators: Cheetahs, owls, gila monsters, raccoons
   Prey: antelopes, mice, eggs, birds, rats, grapes, nuts, crickets, and small mammals

7. commensalism

8. mutualism

9. Answer may vary but should include any relationship in which one organism benefits and the other is harmed.

10. Answers may vary but should include an y description of behavior that helps an animal survive.

11. Innate: Dolphins are able to swim at birth. Learned: Dolphins can perform tricks at a trainer's command.

Learning Coach Guide
Lesson 1: Mixtures and Solutions

In this unit, your student will learn about the world of solutions. Knowing about solutions will help prepare your student for basic chemistry, where knowledge of solutes and solvents are the cornerstone of chemical reactions. As your student learns about solutions, be sure that he uses the terms solute and solvent correctly, and that he understands the difference between a mixture and a solution.

Solutions are mixtures in which one substance dissolves into another with no change to the chemical properties of either substance. Your student will combine different substances with water to determine which make water solutions.

Lesson Objectives

- Define a *substance* as anything that contains only one kind of molecule.
- Describe a *mixture* as a combination of two or more substances that maintain their individual properties and do not go through a chemical change when mixed.
- Define a *solution* as a mixture in which the substances are completely and evenly mixed down to their individual molecules.
- Recognize that solutions can be made from combinations of gases, liquids, and solids.

PREPARE

Approximate lesson time is 60 minutes.

Materials

For the Student

     What's the Solution?

    cup, plastic - 8 oz.

    measuring spoon - tablespoon

    powdered drink mix - one teaspoon

    sand - one teaspoon

    sugar - one teaspoon

    measuring cup

    oil, cooking - one teaspoon

    pencil

    spoon

    water

Lesson Notes

All matter is made up of invisible particles called *atoms*. Most matter is not made of just one kind of atom, though. Rather, it is made up of a combination of many different kinds of atoms. When atoms combine they often form a *molecule*. In water, for example, two hydrogen atoms have combined with one oxygen atom to make one water molecule. Matter that contains only one kind of molecule is called a *substance*.

When a sample of matter changes size, shape, or states, it goes through a *physical change*. In a physical change, the atoms or molecules in the matter do not change, but the way the they are arranged changes. *Chemical changes* come about when one old bonds between atoms are broken and new ones form. The iron atoms in a nail, for example, will react with the oxygen atoms in air and water to form iron oxide, or rust. Rust is a different form of matter than iron. The atoms of iron combine with hydrogen and oxygen atoms to become iron oxide molecules.

Mixtures

Anything that contains two or more chemical substances is called a *mixture*. When a mixture forms, each substance keeps its own properties. No chemical changes take place. A pile of laundry, for example, is a mixture, but the properties of the individual pieces of clothing do not change. Mixtures do not undergo chemical changes, so you can separate them using a physical process. Mixtures can combine evenly or unevenly.

Solutions

In a solution, the chemical substances mix together completely. If you mix lemonade crystals with water, for example, the crystals dissolve completely into the water. Their atoms do not mix, however, so the molecules themselves do not change. Again, the process is a physical change, not a chemical change. Though most people think of solutions as a combination of liquids and solids, you can make solutions from all types of matter: solids, liquids, and gases.

Solutions can be separated by a method called *evaporation*. If you set the glass of lemonade on the counter, the water will eventually evaporate, leaving the lemonade crystals behind. Evaporation is another type of physical change.

Keywords and Pronunciation

dissolve : To mix completely at the molecular level with another substance. Salt and sugar will completely dissolve in water.

mixture : A combination of two or more substances that do not change chemically when mixed. Trail mix is an example of a mixture.

solution : A mixture in which the substances are completely and evenly mixed, down to their individual molecules. Sugar-water is a solution.

substance : Anything that contains only one type of molecule. Gold is an example of a substance.

TEACH
Activity 1: Mixtures and Solutions (Online)

Instructions

Have your student read through the Explore on his own. Reinforce and explain difficult concepts as needed.

Explore Suggestions:

Screen 4: Look around the kitchen for easy examples of mixtures and solutions. Have your student identify which are solutions and share ideas about how they can be separated. His ideas may be incorrect now, but he can revisit them after he studies solutions further in the unit. Some mixtures to find: soups, yogurt mixed with fruit, salad dressing, and milk.

After this activity, check to see if your student can:

- Define a *substance* as anything that contains only one kind of molecule.
- Describe a *mixture* as a combination of two or more substances that maintain their individual properties and do not go through a chemical change when mixed.
- Define a *solution* as a mixture in which the substances are completely and evenly mixed down to their individual molecules.
- Recognize that solutions can be made from combinations of gases, liquids, and solids.

If your student has difficulty with any of these concepts, you may wish to review the Explore with him and have him explain the key points on each screen.

Activity 2: A Special Kind of Mixture *(Offline)*

Instructions

Teaching:

Your student should be able to complete the investigation independently. Take this opportunity to reinforce the scientific method (questioning, predicting, observing, analyzing, and concluding) with him. Check to see that her hypothesis does not include the words "I think." Have your student describe what is happening to the molecules of the substances he mixes. Use clear cups so he can observe each mixture in detail.

What to Expect:

The sugar and powdered drink mix will form solutions with the water. The sand and cooking oil will not.

Answers:

Scientist Notebook:

1. The variable is the substance mixed with water.

2. The effect is whether or not the substances make a solution.

Analysis:

3. The sugar and powdered drink mix will dissolve completely. You can tell because sugar and powdered drink particles cannot be observed in the water.

4. The sand and cooking oil will not dissolve completely. Sand particles and cooking oil are still visible in the water.

Conclusion:

5. The sugar and powdered drink mix will dissolve completely in water to make a solution.

6. Compare your student's hypothesis to his conclusion.

7. Accept any reasonable investigation ideas.

ASSESS

Lesson Assessment: Mixtures and Solutions *(Offline)*

Students will complete an offline assessment based on the lesson objectives. Print the assessment and have students complete it on their own. Use the answer key to score the assessment, and then enter the results online. The attached answer key is the most current and may not coincide with previously printed guides.

Name _____   Date _____

Assessment Answer Key

1. The illustration shows molecules of two separate substances. Draw how the molecules would look when the substances form a solution.

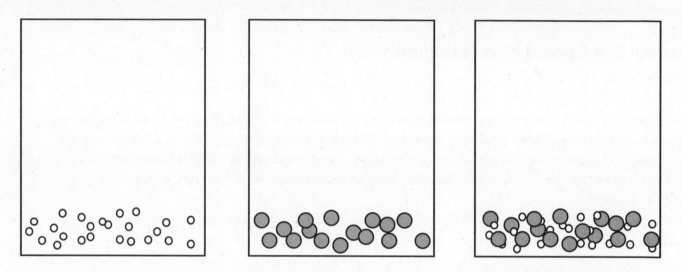

2. Any matter that contains only one kind of molecule is a **substance**_____.

3. Suppose you have a glass of iced tea. You stir in some sugar to make it sweeter. Do you have a solution? **yes**_____

4. Mixing two or more substances in a mixture has _____ on the substances' chemical properties.
   A. a great effect
   B. no effect
   C. disrespect

5. Circle the items below that are solutions:

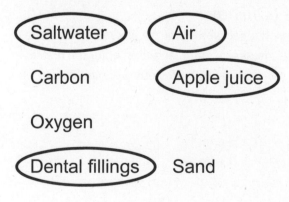

Saltwater   Air

Carbon   Apple juice

Oxygen

Dental fillings   Sand

Learning Coach Guide
Lesson 2: What's Dissolving? Solvents and Solutes

Each solution contains a *solute,* which dissolves, and a *solvent,* which does the dissolving. Identify solvents, solutes, and their resulting solutions by mixing a variety of household substances.

Lesson Objectives

- Define a *solute* as the substance that dissolves in a solution.
- Define a *solvent* as the substance that dissolves a solute to make a solution.
- Identify solute and solvents in different solutions.

PREPARE

Approximate lesson time is 60 minutes.

Materials

For the Student

    💻 Solvent and Solute Mix-Up

        baking soda - 5 mL (1 teaspoon)

        cup, plastic - 8 oz (12)

        measuring spoon

        salt - 5 mL (1 teaspoon)

        soap, liquid - 10 mL (2 teaspoons)

        sugar - 5 mL (teaspoon)

        vinegar - 240 mL (1 cup)

        bowl

        graduated cylinder

        markers - permanent

        oil, cooking - 240 mL (1 cup)

        rubbing alcohol - 240 mL (1 cup)

        spoon

        water - 240 mL (1 cup)

Lesson Notes

A solution is made up of two or more substances, each made of one kind of molecule. The substances in a mixture keep their original properties. When you combine substances to make a mixture, no chemical changes take place. A sugar solution and salt water are good examples of mixtures.

The solution is a special kind of mixture. The substances are completely mixed, right down to their individual molecules. A true solution is the same in every part. Sugar water, for example, tastes the same at the top of the glass as it does at the bottom.

You can't separate a solution in the same way you can somekinds of mixtures--by sorting it or pouring it through a filter. Its particles are so small you cannot see them, and they will not settle to the bottom or float to the top.

In solutions made with large amounts of water or other clear liquids, the particles are so small they let light shine through. Such a solution is transparent. A cranberry cocktail solution, for example, has some color, but it allows rays of light to pass through without bouncing off the particles and scattering around.

Identifying Solvents and Solutes

When you make a solution from a solid and a liquid, the solid seems to disappear into the liquid. In fact, it has dissolved. The dissolved substance is called the *solute.* The substance that does the dissolving is called the *solvent.* Water dissolves so many substances that it is called the *universal solvent.*

In a solution of two substances, there is usually more solvent than solute, although some solutions can have equal amounts. When we name solutions, we typically say the solute first, then the solvent--for example, saltwater, carbonated water, or sugar water.

Tears are a *saline* solution. Saline is called a *universal biological solvent* because it is present inside the human body and the bodies of other organisms. In fact, human saline does not differ greatly from salt concentrations in ocean water.

Keywords and Pronunciation

acetic (uh-SEE-tihk)

acetone (A-suh-tohn)

colloid (KAH-loyd)

solute (SAHL-yoot) : A substance that dissolves in another substance to make a solution. Salt is the solute in saltwater.

solvent : A substance that can dissolve other substances. Water is a solvent of sugar.

TEACH
Activity 1: The "Stuff" of Solutions *(Online)*
Instructions

Explore: Have your student read through the Explore on his own. Reinforce and explain difficult concepts as needed.

Explore Suggestions:

Check your student's understanding by asking the following questions:

1. What's the difference between a mixture and a solution? The substances in a solution blend completely, right down to their molecules. In a mixture, they do not mix down to their individual molecules.
2. Why can't you separate a solution with a filter? The particles are too small.
3. Imagine a mixture of vinegar and spices in which the spices have all sunk to the bottom. How does this tell you that the mixture is not a solution? In a solution, particles will be evenly mixed and won't sink to the bottom.
4. What do we call the substance that dissolves? The solute.
5. What do we call the substance that does the dissolving? The solvent.

Have your student examine labels for ingredients in some of the following solutions. Have him try to identify the solute and solvent for each. Supervise him around any dangerous chemicals.

lemonade

carbonated water

rubbing alcohol

fruit punch

bleach

air freshener

chocolate milk

food coloring

mouthwash

liquid soap

antifreeze

After this activity, check to see if your student can:

- Define a *solute* as the substance that dissolves in a solution.
- Define a *solvent* as the substance that dissolves a solute to make a solution.

If your student has difficulty with any of these concepts, you may wish to review the Explore with him and have him explain the key points on each screen.

Activity 2: Solvents and Solutes Mix-Up *(Offline)*

Instructions

Teaching:

Assist your student in completing the investigation, paying attention to safety. Take this opportunity to reinforce the scientific method--questioning, predicting, observing, analyzing, and concluding--with your student. Use clear cups so he can observe each mixture in detail. Encourage your student to observe each mixture closely, looking for settled particles or "feeling" the undissolved solute on the spoon when he stirs the solution.

What to Expect:

It is important to let each mixture settle before making observations. In most cases, the solute will either dissolve or not dissolve. Mix the baking soda and vinegar over the sink. The chemical reactions caused by mixing these two substances results in fizzing and overflow.

Answers to Solvent and Solute Mix-Up:

Observations:

Will dissolve:

Salt + soapy water

Salt + vinegar

Sugar + soapy water

Sugar + vinegar

Won't dissolve:

Salt + alcohol

Salt + cooking oil

Sugar + alcohol

Sugar + cooking oil

Baking soda + soapy water

Baking soda + alcohol

Baking soda + cooking oil

Baking soda + vinegar

Scientist Notebook:
If the solutes are kept the same for any set of experiments, then the variable is the type of solvents.

Analysis:
Salt + soapy water, salt + vinegar, sugar + soapy water, and sugar + vinegar have completely dissolved solutes.

Salt + alcohol, salt + cooking oil, sugar + alcohol, sugar + cooking oil, baking soda + soapy water, baking soda + alcohol, baking soda + cooking oil, and baking soda + vinegar do not have solutes that are completely dissolved.

Conclusion:
Check to make sure your student compares his results to his hypothesis.
You can tell that a solute has completely dissolved when you do not see it either floating or settling to the bottom of the mixture.

Safety

Have your student wear safety goggles while doing this activity. Caution your student never to taste or inhale anything that is part of a Science lesson unless you have told him it is safe to do so. Do not have him taste or inhale any of the solvents.

ASSESS

Lesson Assessment: What's Dissolving? Solvents and Solutes (*Online*)

Students will complete an offline assessment based on the lesson objectives. Print the assessment and have students complete it on their own. Use the answer key to score the assessment, and then enter the results online. The attached answer key is the most current and may not coincide with previously printed guides.

Lesson Assessment Answer Key

What's Dissolving? Solvents and Solutes

1. a solute

2. a solvent

3. Solutes: salt, sugar, baking soda
   Solvents: soapy water, rubbing alcohol, cooking oil, and vinegar

4. Solutes: sugar, salt, lemon drink mix
   Solvents: water, water, water

Learning Coach Guide
Lesson 3: Separating Solutions

Solutions are not as easy to separate as simple mixtures. Your student will learn about separating solutions and try three methods of separating solutions.

Lesson Objectives

- Describe ways to separate solutions, such as evaporation, chromatography, and distillation.

PREPARE

Approximate lesson time is 60 minutes.

Advance Preparation

- You will need colored candy-coated chocolate for this activity.

Materials

For the Student

    ⌨ Evaporation and Distillation

        cup, plastic - 8 oz.

        household item - pot holder

        pot with lid

        sugar - 60 mL (1/4 cup)

        bowl

        heat source

        spoon

        water - 240 mL (1 cup)

    ⌨ The Makeup of Markers

        cup, plastic (4)

        household item - coffee filters (4)

        marker, black water soluble - blue, green and brown

        pencil

        rubbing alcohol

        ruler, metric

        scissors

        jar - 1 gallon wide-mouth

        water - preferably distilled

📖 Candy Chromatography

coffee filter (4)

food - 4 colors of colored candy

food - candy-coated candy

salt - (1 gram or approximately 1/6 teaspoon)

markers - black

toothpicks

water - (1 liter or approximately 4.25 cups)

Lesson Notes

The substances that make up a mixture keep their original properties even when they are mixed; therefore, it is possible to separate the substances in a mixture. In this lesson, your student will experiment with separating solutions using evaporation, distillation, and chromatography.

Separating Simple Mixtures

There are several simple ways of separating liquid-solid mixtures and solid-solid mixtures.

- *Decanting* - An easy way to separate a liquid from a solid that has settled to the bottom of a container is to gently pour off the liquid, leaving the solid behind. This method of separation is called decanting.
- *Filtering* - You can filter some solid mixtures, such as sand and pebbles, through a screen. The small grains of sand will fall through the screen and the larger pebbles will stay on top.
- *Using a magnet* - Some mixtures separate easily if you stir them with a magnet. In a mixture such as sand and iron filings, the magnet will attract the iron away from the sand.

Separating Solutions

Mixtures that are solutions cannot be separated mechanically because they are made up of very tiny particles. You can't decant solutions, filter them, or use a magnet to separate them. You must use other processes to separate solutions.

- *Evaporation* - One common method for separating liquid solutions is by evaporation. You can easily recover one of the components of a solution such as saltwater with this technique. The water evaporates and leaves the salt crystals behind.
- *Distillation* - Another way to separate liquid solutions is with distillation. The process of distillation, in this case called fractional distillation, is based on the fact that liquids have different boiling points. Water boils at 100 degrees C, but not every liquid boils at this temperature. Ethanol (ethyl alcohol), for example, boils at a lower temperature--78.5 degrees C. By heating a mixture to about 90 degrees C, the ethanol will become a vapor and later can be recovered by cooling. (Caution: This procedure should be done only by scientists with special equipment in a laboratory).

You can also use distillation to separate solutions made of more than two liquids. The closer the boiling points of the liquids, however, the trickier the distillation process, because both liquids will evaporate at nearly the same time.

- *Chromatography* - Chromatography is yet another method for separating solutions. This process relies on the fact that the molecules of certain substances are attracted to the molecules of other substances.

People use paper chromatography to separate the dyes that make up an ink solution. They first place ink on absorbent paper. They then place the paper in a solvent such as water or ethanol. The molecules of some of the ink dyes are attracted to the solvent molecules, and they travel up the paper along with the solvent by a process called capillary action.

Different dyes travel up paper at different rates, so they separate as they move up. A dye that is more strongly attracted to the solvent than to the paper will travel faster and move farther up the paper. A dye that is more strongly attracted to the paper than to the solvent will travel travel less far, because its molecules tend to "stick" to the paper molecules.

Keywords and Pronunciation

centrifuge (SEN-trih-fyooj)

chromatography (kroh-muh-TAH-gruh-fee)

desalination (dee-sa-lih-NAY-shuhn)

distillation : A way of separating liquid substances in a solution that involves heating a liquid and condensing the vapors or gases that form. We used distillation to purify the water.

evaporation : A way of separating substances in a solution that involves heating a liquid to a gas then collecting the leftover solute. Evaporation takes place when you heat water to the boiling point.

paper chromatography : A way of identifying the components of a mixture by treating them with a solvent then observing how they travel on absorbent paper. When you use black ink in paper chromatography, a rainbow of colors will travel up the paper.

solute (SAHL-yoot) : A substance that dissolves in another substance to make a solution. Salt is the solute in saltwater.

TEACH

Activity 1: Let's Separate Solutions *(Online)*

Instructions

Have your student read through the Explore on his own. Reinforce and explain difficult concepts as needed.

Explore Suggestions:

Check your student's understanding by asking the questions below:

1. Why are solutions more difficult to separate by mechanically or by filtering? (They are made up of very tiny particles that can't be filtered or removed by hand)

2. Chromatography does not use evaporation to separate solutions. It relies on the attraction of _____ to a solid and a liquid. (molecules)

After this activity, check to see if your student can:

- Describe ways to separate solutions, such as evaporation, chromatography, and distillation.

If your student has difficulty with any of these concepts, you may wish to review the Explore with him and have him explain the key points on each screen.

Safety

Caution your student not to try the distillation process on ethanol and water. This is a very dangerous procedure that only scientists should perform in their laboratory.

Activity 2: Evaporation and Distillation *(Offline)*

Instructions

Teaching:

Talk with your student about what will happen during the evaporation and distillation activities. Reinforce that the result will be separation of the water and sugar solution.

What to Expect:

Both evaporation and distillation will take a significant amount of time to complete. If you decide to wait it out, what will be left is sugar in the bottom of the cup and pan. Your student should understand that evaporation and distillation are two ways to separate solutions. He should be able to describe the process involved in both methods and should recognize how distillation and evaporation differ. Evaporation allows water to escape into the air as vapor; distillation involves collecting the water vapor, allowing it to condense, and then collecting it.

Safety

Use extreme caution when working with boiling water. Never leave your student unattended near hot or boiling water.

Activity 3: The Makeup of Markers *(Offline)*

Instructions

Teaching:

Talk with your student about how paper chromatography works. The alcohol-water solution moves through the paper because of capillary action, separating the colors of the ink. Each ink color travels different distances on the paper depending on the attraction it has for the paper (a solid) or the solvent (a liquid). Before extracting ink from the markers, have your student predict what colors might show up on the paper.

Troubleshooting:

Certain markers may be more difficult to separate than others. Try a variety of marker brands if yours does not separate into different colors. The markers will not separate right away. Have your student observe the paper for about 5 minutes.

What to Expect:

The paper will soak up the alcohol-water solvent and separate the inks into different colors. Your student should understand that paper chromatography is a third way to separate solutions.

Answers:

1. The marker dots separated into different colors.
2. Check to see that your student's observations are accurate.
3. Check to see that your student's observations are accurate.

ASSESS

Lesson Assessment: Separating Solutions (*Online*)

Students will complete an offline assessment based on the lesson objectives. Print the assessment and have students complete it on their own. Use the answer key to score the assessment, and then enter the results online. The attached answer key is the most current and may not coincide with previously printed guides.

TEACH
Activity 4. Optional: Pollution Solution *(Offline)*
Instructions
Teaching:

Talk about some real-world situations in which separating solutions may be important. Separating particles in the air from water will give clues to the kinds of pollution in your area.

What to Expect:

Your student should find various types of particulate matter collected in the jars. Discuss what is and what is not pollution; for example, leaves and bugs are not pollution.

Activity 5. Optional: Candy Chromatography *(Offline)*
Instructions
Teaching:

Review with your student about how paper chromatography works. The salt-water solution moves through the paper because of capillary action, separating the colors of the dye. Each dye color travels different distances on the paper depending on the attraction it has for the paper (a solid) or the solvent (a liquid). Before extracting dye from the candies, have your student predict what colors might show up on the paper.

Troubleshooting:

Use colors that you know are made from more than one type of dye, for example brown, orange, or green. Avoid adding too much water to the cup as you extract the dyes from the candies. The dye should be dark and concentrated, not watery. The dye may be difficult to concentrate in the spot on the filter paper. You can carefully use an eyedropper, but do not allow the dye outside of the circle on the paper.

If the dyes do not separate on the filter paper, try the activity again using less water to extract the dye. Refer to the Explore section to review how chromatography works and how the colors should look when separated.

What to Expect:

The paper will soak up the saltwater solvent and should separate the dyes. Your student should understand that paper chromatography is a third way to separate solutions

Answers:

Check to see that your student's observations match the results of the experiment.

Lesson Assessment Answer Key

Separating Solutions

1. by using either evaporation or distillation

2. chromatography

3. Answers may vary but should include: boil the water, then collect the vapor and allow it to condense back into water. You can then pour the water into a separate container and the salt will be left behind in the pot.

4. Molly found no water, but there was salt in the bottom of the container. The water had evaporated.

Learning Coach Guide
Lesson 4: Dissolving Solutions Quickly

Your student will explore more in-depth properties of solutions. The rate at which a solute dissolves in a solution depends on the relationship betwen the solute's *surface area* and the surrounding solvent. A larger surface area will result in a greater dissolving rate, as will shaking or stirring.

Lesson Objectives

- Describe two ways to increase the rate at which solids dissolve in liquids (by crushing them into smaller pieces and by stirring).
- Recognize that breaking up a solute into smaller pieces increases its surface area.

PREPARE

Approximate lesson time is 60 minutes.

Advance Preparation

- If you don't already have it, you will need 12 sugar cubes for this activity.

Materials

For the Student

🖳 Grind, Shake, and Stir

household item - container with lids (2)

household item - large wooden spoon or similar utensil

household item - plastic sandwich bag

sugar cube (12)

graduated cylinder

paper, notebook

spoon (2)

timer

water - 480 mL (2 cups)

Lesson Notes

When you stir a solid into a liquid, it usually takes some time for the solid to dissolve completely. How fast it dissolves is related to how much of its surface area is in contact with the liquid. An object's *surface area* is the sum of all the outside surfaces of the object.

When you break up a solid, you increase its surface area. And the more surface area the liquid can contact, the faster the solid will dissolve. In other words, a lot of small pieces will dissolve faster than one large piece. A sugar cube and water can illustrate the concept of a solid dissolving in a liquid. A crushed sugar cube has a larger surface area than an intact cube; therefore, the crushed sugar cube will dissolve in water more quickly. If you crush the sugar cube, all the sugar grains that were on the inside can be exposed immediately to the water.

Shaking and Stirring Speeds Up the Rate of Dissolution

When a whole sugar cube starts to dissolve in water, the water molecules surround the sugar molecules, and the sugar molecules begin to mix with the water molecules. Since molecules are constantly in motion, more and more sugar dissolves until lots of sugar molecules are concentrated around the cube. At this point, a process called diffusion begins. In *diffusion,* molecules dissolving in a liquid move from areas of high concentration to areas of low concentration. The sugar molecules in the area of high concentration near the cube begin moving away. As the dissolved sugar molecules move away from the cube, more molecules break away from it and take their place. The process also takes place in reverse, so there is a constant interplay between solute and solvent.

Diffusion generally happens slowly, but shaking or stirring can speed up the process because it moves the sugar molecules away from the sugar cube.

In many cases, solids dissolve faster if you shake, rather than stir, a solution. The shaking disperses the solute more rapidly into the solvent than stirring does. Therefore, more solvent molecules can act on the solute.

Keywords and Pronunciation

solute (SAHL-yoot) : A substance that dissolves in another substance to make a solution. Salt is the solute in saltwater.

surface area : The amount of space the outer face of an object takes up. The six surfaces of the block of wood took up 600 millimeters squared of space, so the surface area is 600 millimeters squared.

TEACH
Activity 1: Slow or Speedy? What's the Secret? *(Online)*
Instructions
Have your student read through the Explore on his own. Reinforce and explain difficult concepts as needed.
Explore Suggestions:
Check your student's understanding by asking the following questions:
1. What do we mean when we say that breaking up an object makes the object's surface area bigger? (An object that's been broken up has more surface area exposed, so the total amount of all the outer surfaces of the object is bigger.)
After this activity, check to see if your student can:
· Describe two ways to increase the rate at which solids dissolve in liquids (by crushing them into smaller pieces and by stirring).
· Recognize that breaking up a solute into smaller pieces increases its surface area.
If your student has difficulty with any of these concepts, you may wish to review the Explore with him and have him explain the key points on each screen.

Activity 2: Grind, Shake, and Stir *(Offline)*
Instructions
Teaching:
Talk about surface area. The larger the surface area of a solute that comes in contact with a solvent, the faster the solute will dissolve. Note that grinding the sugar cubes will change how fast they dissolve, but it will not change how much will dissolve. The same amount of sugar will dissolve from the whole sugar cube as from the crushed one.

Troubleshooting:

Make sure the sugar is ground into a very fine powder. Assist your student in placing both types of sugar into the water at the same time.

What to Expect:

The crushed sugar cubes will dissolve faster than the whole sugar cubes. Your student should understand that this is because the crushed sugar has a larger surface area. Your student should also understand that shaking and stirring the solutions speeds up the dissolving rate as well.

Answers:

1. The crushed sugar cubes dissolved faster.
2. Your student's results should match what he has read and heard about surface area.
3. Shaking and stirring allows the molecules of solvent to come into contact with the solute more often.
4. Shaking or stirring the powder in water would dissolve it quickly.

ASSESS

Lesson Assessment: Dissolving Solutions Quickly (*Offline*)

Students will complete an online assessment based on the lesson objectives. The assessment will be scored by the computer. The attached answer key is the most current and may not coincide with previously printed guides.

Learning Coach Guide
Lesson 5: Solubility

Solutes differ in how much can dissolve in a specific solvent. Some substances are *soluble*, meaning they mostly dissolve in specific solvents. Some are *somewhat soluble*, and only partially dissolve. Still others are *insoluble* and dissolve in very small amounts in a specific solvent. Changing the temperature of the solvent can increase or decrease the solubility of substances as well. Your student will compare substances for solubility, and then observe the effects of increasing temperature while creating a salt water and sugar water solution.

Lesson Objectives

- Recognize that increasing the temperature of a solvent usually increases the rate at which a solute dissolves.
- Recognize that increasing the temperature of a solvent can change the solubility of a solid solute.
- Define *solubility* as the maximum total amount of a solid that can dissolve into a given quantity of a particular solvent at a given temperature.
- Recognize that not all substances dissolve in a given quantity of water in the same amounts.
- Classify substances as soluble, insoluble, and somewhat soluble.

PREPARE

Approximate lesson time is 60 minutes.

Materials

For the Student
    💻 Is It Soluble?

      cornstarch - 10 mL (2 tsp.)

      cup, plastic - 8 oz. (6)

      measuring spoon

      sand - 10 mL (2 tsp.)

      sugar - 10 mL (2 tsp.)

      funnel

      graduated cylinder

      paper towels (3)

      spoon

      water

⊟ How Many Spoonfuls to Saturation?

jar - glass (4)

pot with lid

salt

sugar

thermometer, Celsius/Fahrenheit

heat source

measuring cup

water - 400 mL

Lesson Notes

Dissolving Solutes by Applying Heat

Besides crushing, stirring, and shaking, there is another way to speed up the process by which most solid solutes dissolve in solvents: raising the solvent's temperature. Raising the temperature also changes how much solute can be dissolved in the solvent.

Solubility and Saturation

When a solvent has dissolved as much of a specific solute as it can, we say the solution is *saturated*. This maximum amount of solute in a specific amount of solvent is called the *solubility* of the solute. Solubility is often expressed as grams of solute that can dissolve in 100 grams of solvent.

Solubility changes with temperature, so temperature must always be specified when discussing solubility. At room temperature (20 °C), the most sugar that can dissolve in 100 grams of water is 204 grams. But at 60 °C, about 287 grams of sugar can dissolve. So when we raise the temperature, the sugar's solubility increases.

Not all solutes dissolve equally in a particular solvent, because the molecules of solvents and solutes interact differently. For example, the same amounts of salt and sugar will not dissolve in the same amount of water. Sugar is more soluble in water than is salt.

Not only do different substances have different solubilities in water, they also have different solubilities in different solvents. Salt, for example, has one solubility in water and another solubility in a solvent like acetone or ethanol.

Soluble, Insoluble, and Somewhat Soluble

When a lot of solute can dissolve in a solvent, we say the substance is *soluble*. If a substance only dissolves a small amount in a solvent, we say it is *insoluble*. Some substances lie between the two and are described as *somewhat soluble*.

Keywords and Pronunciation

acetone (A-suh-tohn)

saturated : Dissolving the greatest possible amount of a substance in a solution. The liquid in a hummingbird feeder is a supersaturated solution of sugar and water.

solubility (sahl-yuh-BIH-luh-tee) : How much solute can be dissolved in a solvent at a given temperature. The solubility of the sugar increased when we raised the temperature.

soluble (SAHL-yuh-buhl) : Able to be dissolved. Sugar is soluble in water.

solute (SAHL-yoot) : A substance that dissolves in another substance to make a solution. Salt is the solute in saltwater.

TEACH
Activity 1: Why Doesn't It All Dissolve? *(Online)*
Instructions
Have your student read through the Explore on his own. Reinforce and explain difficult concepts as needed.

Explore Suggestions:

Screen 4: Check your student's understanding of the concept of *saturation.* When a solution is *saturated,* it means there is no room for more of the solute to dissolve in the solvent. The solution is said to have reached its *saturation point.*

Screen 5: Using the information on the graph, ask your student to tell you at what temperature showing on the graph is sugar most soluble.

After this activity, check to see if your student can:
- Recognize that increasing the temperature of a solvent usually increases the rate at which a solute dissolves.
- Recognize that increasing the temperature of a solvent can change the solubility of a solid solute.
- Define *solubility* as the maximum total amount of a solid that can dissolve into a given quantity of a particular solvent at a given temperature.
- Recognize that not all substances dissolve in a given quantity of water in the same amounts.

If your student has difficulty with any of these concepts, you may wish to review the Explore with him and have him explain the key points on each screen.

Activity 2: Soluble, Insoluble, and Somewhat Soluble *(Offline)*
Instructions
Teaching:

Discuss the definition of solubility. The mass of a solute that can dissolve in a particular solvent is that solute's solubility at a specific temperature. Some substances are not soluble, while some are only partially soluble.

What to Expect:

The sugar + water solution should pass directly through the filter with no remaining solute. Sand will not pass through the filter and is insoluble. Some of the cornstarch will remain in the filter as the rest passes through, thereby making it somewhat soluble. Direct your student to observe the filter and the appearance of the water after filtration. He should understand that some substances are soluble while others are not.

Answers:

Scientist Notebook:

The variable is the different solutes.

Conclusion:

1. The sugar was soluble, the sand was insoluble, and the cornstarch was somewhat soluble.

2. If the solute did not pass entirely through the filter, then the substance was not soluble. If there was some solute in the water after filtering, then the substance was either soluble or somewhat soluble.

3. Your student should check his results with his hypothesis.

4. Allow the water to evaporate, and then sugar should be left behind.

Activity 3: Solubility and Temperature *(Offline)*
Instructions
Teaching:

Discuss how changing temperature changes solubility and what is meant by "saturated". When no more solute can dissolve into a solution, that solution is saturated. Discuss what a saturated solution might look like, for example visible particles of solute settling to the bottom.

Troubleshooting:

Transparent cups, or mugs that can hold warm water may be substituted for the glass jars. For this experiment, it is fine to measure the volume of sugar used. Instead of a cylinder, you can use a measuring spoon and count spoonfuls of solute added, then calculate the mL used. Assist your student in making the line graph.

Look for signs of saturation by spooning out some of the solution. If salt or sugar is visible on the spoon, then it is saturated. You can also use the solubility graph for salt and sugar in the Explore as a guide to show how much of each solute will dissolve into the temperature of water you are using.

What to Expect:

More sugar and salt will dissolve in the hot water than in the cold. However, much more sugar will dissolve than salt- sugar is much more soluble. After completing the line graph, your student should understand that as the temperature of a solvent increases, more solute can be dissolved in it. Your student should also understand that the solute will dissolve more quickly in the warmer liquid than the cold.

Answers:

Conclusion:

1. Sugar is the most soluble.
2. The temperature of the solvent and the amount of solute added will determine when a solution is saturated.

Safety

Never leave your student unattended near a stove, oven, or microwave. Use extreme caution when working with boiling water. Never leave your student unattended near hot or boiling water.

ASSESS

Lesson Assessment: Solubility (*Online*)

Students will complete an online assessment based on the lesson objectives. The assessment will be scored by the computer. The attached answer key is the most current and may not coincide with previously printed guides.

Learning Coach Guide
Lesson 6: Concentrations

Your student will focus on another property of solutions--*concentration.* Explore the difference between *concentrated* and *diluted,* then create solutions with different degrees of concentration.

Lesson Objectives

- Compare the concentrations of different solutions and describe them as concentrated or dilute.
- State the concentration of solutions as the number of grams of solute per 100 grams of solvent.
- Recognize that, at a given temperature, a solution is saturated when the maximum amount of solute has been dissolved into the solvent.

PREPARE

Approximate lesson time is 60 minutes.

Advance Preparation

- You will need to wait for a juice solution to freeze to complete this activity. You may choose to start the activity early then return to it during the lesson, or to do the activity during the lesson and return to it later. Have your student complete the Not Too Sweet: Solution Dilution lab sheet up to the Observations section, then finish the lab sheet after the solution has completely frozen.

Materials

For the Student

    📖 Not Too Sweet: Solution Dilution

    cup, plastic - 8 oz. (6)

    freezing source

    household item - ice cube tray

    powdered drink mix - one packet

    sugar - 480 mL (2 cups)

    bowl - or pitcher

    graduated cylinder

    markers

    measuring cup

    spoon

    tape, masking

    toothpicks (6)

    water

    food - oil-based salad dressing

    juice

    milk

    flashlight

    glass, drinking (3)

Lesson Notes

Solubility is the mass, in grams, of a solute that can dissolve in 100 grams of solvent.

When a solvent cannot dissolve any more solute, the solution it is said to be *saturated.* In a saturated solution, any extra solute that won't dissolve often collects at the bottom or top of the solvent. When a solvent has not yet reached its saturation point, it is said to be *unsaturated.*

Concentrations and Dilutes

The amount of solid dissolved in a solvent is called the solution's *concentration.* The concentration of a solution at any given temperature is the number of grams of solute dissolved in 100 grams of solvent.

A concentrated solution has a relatively large of amount of solute. A *diluted* solution has a relatively small amount of solute. The terms *concentrated* and *diluted,* though useful for comparing the approximate strengths of solutions, are not exact descriptions.

Chemists often need to know exact concentrations before they mix solutions together. Some chemical reactions will take place only when solutions have a certain concentration. A more scientific way to state the concentration of a solution is by the number of grams of solute dissolved in 100 grams of solvent. Another way is as the percent of solute to solvent. The labels of juices, for example, may state that the solution contains 40 percent juice and 60 percent water.

Suspensions and Colloids

A *suspension* is a mixture in which one substance is spread throughout another, but you can still see the particles (or overall cloudiness) of the substance. Oil-and-vinegar salad dressing is an example of a suspension. Soil and water is another example, as moving water carries "suspended" sediments.

A *colloid* is a mixture in which some solid particles do not dissolve, but are so small they do not settle to the bottom. The particles are too tiny to see, but they are larger than molecules. Homogenized milk, butter, ice cream, chocolate, and hair conditioner are all examples of colloids.

Keywords and Pronunciation

colloid (KAH-loyd) : a heterogeneous mixture from which the suspended particles do not settle out

concentrated : Containing a large amount of solute. The juice in the frozen section of the grocery store is very concentrated, and we have to add water before we can drink it.

concentration : The amount of one substance dissolved in another. Weak and strong tea have different concentrations.

diluted : Containing very little solute. Weak tea is a very diluted solution and contains more water than tea.

solubility (sahl-yuh-BIH-luh-tee) : How much solute can be dissolved in a solvent at a given temperature. The solubility of the sugar increased when we raised the temperature.

solute (SAHL-yoot) : A substance that dissolves in another substance to make a solution. Salt is the solute in saltwater.

TEACH

Activity 1: Concentrating on Solutions *(Online)*

Instructions

Have your student read through the Explore on his own. Reinforce and explain difficult concepts as needed.

Explore Suggestions:

Screen 2: Research some areas where concentrations of solutions are important such as in film development, milk-fat concentrations for babies, and in cooking.

Screen 3: Name That Solution Answers: maple syrup, honey, vanilla, vinegar

After this activity, check to see if your student can:

- Compare the concentrations of different solutions and describe them as *concentrated* or *dilute*.
- State the concentration of solutions as the number of grams of solute per 100 grams of solvent.
- Recognize that, at a given temperature, a solution is saturated when the maximum amount of solute has been dissolved into the solvent.

If your student has difficulty with any of these concepts, you may wish to review the Explore with him and have him explain the key points on each screen.

Activity 2: Not Too Sweet *(Offline)*

Instructions

Teaching:

Review concentration and dilution. Concentration is the amount of solid dissolved in a solvent. A concentrated solution is near its maximum concentration. A diluted solution has a small amount of solute, such as weak lemonade or tea. You can often tell differences in concentrations of solutions by color or by taste. Encourage your student to look for color changes in the solutions as he dilutes them with water.

Troubleshooting:

The solution in Cube 6 may appear lighter or not taste as sweet. This does not mean that no drink mix or sugar remains in the solution. As water is added and the drink is stirred, the drink and sugar molecules continue to spread evenly throughout the water. When enough water is added, they become far enough apart to appear invisible because of their small size.

What to Expect:

From Cube 1 to Cube 6, the solutions will appear lighter in color and will not taste as sweet. Your student should understand that adding water to the solutions dilutes them, which means there is less solute per the amount of solute, or less sugar and drink mix per the amount of water in each cube.

Answers:

Another way to investigate concentration, other than tasting, is to look for a color change.

Observations:

1. The color of the cubes becomes lighter from cube 1 - 6.
2. Yes there still would be powdered drink mix and sugar in the cube. As more water was added, their molecules would have spread out, eventually spreading so far that they appear invisible. The molecules are still in the cube, though.
3. The cubes taste less sweet from cube 1 - 6.
4. Yes, there is still some sugar in all of the cups.
5. Yes, this test could have been done by just observing and tasting the juice.

ASSESS

Lesson Assessment: Concentrations (*Online*)

Students will complete an online assessment based on the lesson objectives. The assessment will be scored by the computer. The attached answer key is the most current and may not coincide with previously printed guides.

TEACH
Activity 3. Optional: New Mixtures: Colloids and Suspensions *(Offline)*
Instructions

Teaching:

Introduce two new types of mixtures: colloids and suspensions. Their main difference is particle size. The particles in colloids are small enough to mix evenly and stay mixed, but do not dissolve. They are made of clumps of molecules, rather than individual molecules. Suspensions contain particles that are too large to dissolve and stay mixed. Particles in a suspension will sink to the bottom of the mixture.

What to Expect:

Your student will make some general observations about the three mixtures. The particles will settle only in the salad dressing, the suspension. Shining a beam of light through each mixture will produce different results, called the *Tyndall Effect.* Light will not be visible in the solution because the particles are too small to scatter light. Light will be visible in the colloid because its particles are large enough to reflect light. Particles in a suspension will not let light through.

Your student should understand that solutions, colloids, and suspensions differ based on particle size, which affects how they transmit or reflect light.

Learning Coach Guide
Lesson 7: Unit Review and Assessment

To conclude the unit on the chemistry of solutions, your student will review key terms, then take an assessment.

Lesson Objectives

- Describe ways to separate solutions, such as evaporation, chromatography, and distillation.
- Describe a *mixture* as a combination of two or more substances that maintain their individual properties and do not go through a chemical change when mixed.
- Define a *solution* as a mixture in which the substances are completely and evenly mixed down to their individual molecules.
- Recognize that solutions can be made from combinations of gases, liquids, and solids.
- Define a *solute* as the substance that dissolves in a solution.
- Define a *solvent* as the substance that dissolves a solute to make a solution.
- Describe two ways to increase the rate at which solids dissolve in liquids (by crushing them into smaller pieces and by stirring).
- Recognize that increasing the temperature of a solvent usually increases the rate at which a solute dissolves.
- Recognize that increasing the temperature of a solvent can change the solubility of a solid solute.
- Recognize that not all substances dissolve in a given quantity of water in the same amounts.
- Classify substances as soluble, insoluble, and somewhat soluble.
- Compare the concentrations of different solutions and describe them as concentrated or dilute.
- Identify solute and solvents in different solutions.

PREPARE

Approximate lesson time is 60 minutes.

Materials

For the Student

    💻 Crossword Chemistry

    pencil

For the Adult

    💻 Crossword Chemistry Answer Key

Lesson Notes

A *mixture* is two or more substances that become physically mixed but whose molecules do not undergo a chemical change. A *solution* is a mixture in which the molecules are evenly mixed and remain completely mixed over time--nothing settles out. Solutions can be of many types, such as liquid-liquid, liquid-gas, or even solid-solid, such as brass.

Your student should understand the basic terminology of solutions. The smaller portion of a solution is called a *solute*. The substance making up the majority of the solution is called the *solvent*. The solute is what is being dissolved, and the solvent is the substance doing the dissolving. The amount of solute in a solvent is its *solubility,* which is affected by temperature.

Even though the molecules of a solution are mixed, you can separate them. *Evaporation* of a liquid solvent will leave a residue of the solute, such as the salt crystals left at the bottom of a pan. *Distillation* (fractional distillation) is another effective way to separate two liquids. *Chromatography* uses the different affinities that a mixture has for paper or other material to separate the component parts of a solution.

TEACH
Activity 1: Crossword Chemistry *(Offline)*
Instructions
Teaching:

Take some time to talk over the new things your student learned about solutions during the unit. Allow your student to return to any lessons or activities from the unit to complete the unit review.

What to Expect:

Your student should be able to complete the crossword independently by referring to previous lessons.

Answers:

See Crossword Chemistry Answer Key.

ASSESS
Unit Assessment: Chemistry of Solutions (*Offline*)

Students will complete an offline Unit Assessment. Print the assessment and have students complete it on their own. Use the answer key to score the assessment, and then enter the results online. The attached answer key is the most current and may not coincide with previously printed guides.

TEACH
Activity 2. Optional: ZlugQuest Measurement *(Online)*

Name _____   Date _____

Crossword Chemistry Answer Key

Name _____ Date _____

Chemistry of Solutions Unit Assessment

1. Circle the statements that describe a mixture. There is more than one true statement.

   A mixture produces a completely new substance.
   (A mixture can be separated by a filter. **(1 pt.)**)
   (In a mixture, no chemical changes take place. **(1 pt.)**)
   In a mixture, the properties of every substance change.
   (In a mixture, molecules can mix, but do not change completely. **(1 pt.)**)
   A mixture can be separated only by chemical ways.

2. A __**(2 pts.)** solution__ is a mixture in which the substances that make it up are completely and evenly mixed right down to their individual molecules.

3. Study the illustration. In the third container, draw how these molecules would look when mixed in a solution. **(4 pts.)**

4. Next to each solution write the phases of matter (solid, liquid, or gas) that make it up. **(1 pt. for each blank, 8 pts. total)**

   A. soft drink __liquid__ + __gas__.
   B. air __gas__ + __gas__.
   C. mud __solid__ + __liquid__.
   D. steel (metal and iron) __solid__ + __solid__.

Chemistry of Solutions Unit Assessment

5. A substance that dissolves in a solution is called the (2 pts.)   solute .

6. A group of students attempt to make solutions with water and the following solids: sugar, sand, and salt. After mixing the solutions, they poured each through a filter. The sugar and salt passed through the filter, but the sand did not. Tell whether each solid was soluble or insoluble. **(1 pt. each, 3 pts. total)**

<u>**Soluble**</u>   <u>**Insoluble**</u>

sugar   **sand**

salt

7. One of the students suggests using a different solvent to make the solution. Suggest two more solvents to use. **(4 pts.)**   **Answers may vary but should include two other liquids that are capable of dissolving, such as soap, rubbing alcohol, or vinegar, but not cooking oil.**

8. After mixing the sugar and water, one student wanted to separate them again. Name two ways to do this. **(4 pts.)**   **The student could evaporate or distill the solution.**

9. Read the list of solutions. Tell whether each substance in the solution is a solute or a solvent. **(1 pt. each, 6 pts. total)**
   Sugar + water
   water + lemon juice
   Chocolate syrup + milk

<u>**Solute**</u>   <u>**Solvent**</u>

sugar   **water**

chocolate syrup   **milk**

lemon juice

Chemistry of Solutions Unit Assessment

10. Imagine you place a piece of chocolate on your tongue. Which will cause it to dissolve faster, chewing it up into pieces or allowing it to sit on your tongue? **(2 pts.) chewing it up into pieces.**

11. Stirring sugar into tea makes the sugar dissolve more quickly. What effect does stirring have on the molecules of tea and sugar? **(2 pts.) Stirring creates spaces between water molecules into which sugar molecules can dissolve.**

12. Which will dissolve more quickly—sugar in iced tea or in hot tea? **(1 pt.) sugar in hot tea**

Study the graph. It shows the amounts of three different solids that can dissolve in 100g of water between 0 °C and 100 °C.

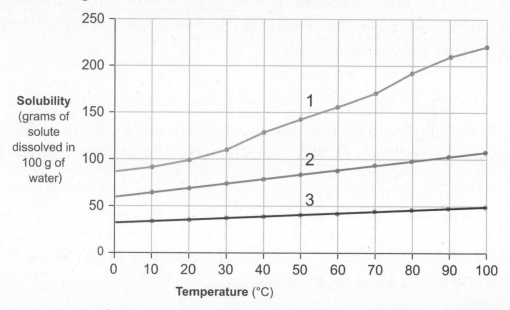

13. Write the solubility of solid 1, 2, and 3 at 50 °C. **(1 pt. each, 3 pts. total) 145g, 80g, 45g**

14. Study solid 1. What happens to its solubility as the water temperature is increased? **(2 pts.) It becomes more soluble. More grams of it can be dissolved in hotter water.**

Chemistry of Solutions Unit Assessment

15. Imagine that solid 1 is sugar and solid 3 is salt. Would you expect the same amount of sugar and salt to dissolve in the same amount of water? Why and why not? **(2 pts.)** No, because not all substances can dissolve in water in the same amounts.

Study the concentration listed on the juice labels, then answer the questions.

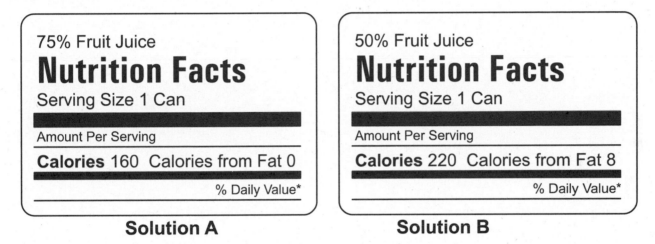

75% Fruit Juice		
Nutrition Facts		
Serving Size 1 Can		

Amount Per Serving

Calories 160 Calories from Fat 0

% Daily Value*

Solution A

50% Fruit Juice		
Nutrition Facts		
Serving Size 1 Can		

Amount Per Serving

Calories 220 Calories from Fat 8

% Daily Value*

Solution B

16. Which solution is more concentrated? **(2 pts.)**   solution A

17. If you could observe only the juices and not the labels, what two things could you do to find out which is concentrated and which is diluted? **(4 pts.)**
You could observe their color or taste them.

Learning Coach Guide
Lesson 1. Optional: Pressure

We come across many types of forces that involve fluids. Air pressure is the force of air molecules pressing on our bodies. Airplanes experience drag and thrust, as well as gravity and lift. A ship floats due to the forces of gravity and the buoyant force of water. By focusing on these forces in fluids, we can make sense of many phenomena we see around us.

Pressure is the force due to weight of air or water pressing over a certain area. Your student will learn the formula for calculating pressure and become familiar with its measurement unit, the *pascal*. You will also demonstrate the effects of changes in air pressure by crushing an aluminum can.

Lesson Objectives

- Explain that atmospheric pressure decreases with height above sea level and water pressure increases with depth below sea level.
- State that a substance that flows--for example, a gas or a liquid--is a *fluid*.
- Describe the forces present in flight: lift, weight, thrust, and drag.
- Define pressure as the force exerted on a surface and recognize that pressure is measured in a unit called the pascal.

PREPARE

Approximate lesson time is 60 minutes.

Materials

For the Student

🖻 Can Crusher: It's no Trick!

baking dish, rectangular - or shallow pie plate

can - empty soda

oven mitt - or tongs

heat source - stove or hot plate

water - cold

🖻 Make a Barometer

clay

plastic bottle - 473 mL

bowl

eyedropper

food coloring

markers - permanent

ruler

straw, drinking

water

Lesson Notes

A layer of air called the *atmosphere* surrounds our planet. Earth's gravity pulls the molecules in the atmosphere down toward the Earth. That is, our atmosphere has weight. This pressure is called *air pressure*, or *atmospheric pressure*. It pushes on everything on the planet. But air pressure pushes in all directions, not just downward from gravity. This is partly because air is a fluid. A fluid is a substance whose molecules move around freely, or flow. Liquids and gases flow, so they are fluids. Air molecules flow all around and bounce into things from all different angles, so air pressure pushes in all directions. A simple example is the air inside a balloon. It pushes on all the inside surface of the balloon, not just downward.

Variations in Air and Water Pressure

Air pressure is not the same everywhere on the planet. When you climb a mountain, you find that the air pressure on top of the mountain is less than the air pressure at the bottom because there are fewer air molecules above you. As you move back toward sea level, air pressure increases because there are more air molecules above you to push on you.

Not only does air have pressure, but water has pressure, too. As you go deeper in the ocean, more and more water molecules push on you from above and around. But water pressure increases much more quickly than air pressure because the molecules in a liquid are closer together than the molecules of a gas. More and more water molecules push against you, so they push with greater force.

Measuring Air Pressure

Air pressure also changes with the weather. Weather forecasters measure air pressure with a barometer. Air pressure can also be measured by determining the force on an area and then dividing it by the size of the surface on which the force is pressing. We write this as pressure = force ÷ area.

A force is just a push or pull. You can measure force with a spring scale. The unit of measurement for expressing force is a newton (N). Area is the total size of a surface. To find area you multiply the length of the surface by the width and express the answer in square meters, or m². When you measure force in newtons and divide it by the area in square meters, the resulting pressure is expressed in pascals (Pa). This unit is named after Blaise Pascal, was the first to show that fluid pressure pressed equally in all directions.

Keywords and Pronunciation

aneroid (A-nuh-royd)

barometer (buh-RAH-muh-tuhr)

Blaise Pascal (blez pahs-KAHL)

fluid : Any substance that flows. Air flows, so air is considered a fluid.

pascal (pahs-KAHL) : A unit of pressure calculated by dividing the force in newtons by the area measured in square meters. Air pressure is measured in pascals.

pressure : The force acting over a given area of a surface. Even though you may not feel it, the air around you is applying pressure on you and everything around you.

TEACH
Activity 1. Optional: Optional Lesson Instructions *(Online)*

Activity 2. Optional: Fluids Put the Pressure On *(Online)*
Instructions
Have your student read through the Explore on her own. Reinforce and explain difficult concepts as needed.

Explore Suggestions:

Screen 2: Find out how the pressure of brake fluid is used to allow a driver to stop a moving vehicle with just one foot.

Screen 3: Look at preparation instructions for packaged foods that involve boiling water. Have your student find out why there are separate instructions for preparing food at high altitudes.

Screen 5: Use a simple illustration to reinforce the concept of pressure with your student. Draw a square and have your student draw arrows representing a force pushing on the outside of the square. The square represents a square meter of space. The arrows represent the force in Newtons pushing on the square. Remember that pressure occurs on all sides of an object.

Screen 6: Use an eyedropper to compare the pressures of air and water. Have your student squeeze an empty eyedropper and observe the force used to squeeze all of the air out. Have her fill it with water and squeeze again, then compare the force used to squeeze all of the water out.

After this activity, check to see if your student can:

- Define pressure as the force exerted on a surface per unit area and recognize that pressure is measured in a unit called a *pascal*.
- Explain that atmospheric pressure decreases with height above sea level while water pressure increases with depth below sea level.
- State that a substance that flows--for example, a gas or a liquid--is a fluid.

If your student has difficulty with any of these concepts, you may wish to review the Explore with her and have her explain the key points on each screen.

Activity 3. Optional: Can Crusher *(Offline)*

Instructions

Teaching:

Talk about pressure. Review the idea that pressure is caused by the movement of molecules in a fluid. Remind your student that when blowing up a balloon, there is air pressure outside the balloon as well as inside. Air pressure outside the balloon pushes on it. This is important to remember during the activity, when air pressure outside the can causes interesting effects because it is higher than the pressure inside the can.

Troubleshooting:

If you are using a stove, the can may be placed directly on the burner. If using a gas stove, do not place the can over direct flame but on the side of the burner. The water in the can will heat quickly.

What to Expect:

As soon as you place the can upside down in the pan, it will be crushed. This is due to the fact that the water heated in the can turned into water vapor, a gas. The water vapor pushes out the air and fills the can. Molecules of gas take up more space than liquid molecules. Turning the can over in the pan of water cools the gas and it condenses to a liquid. The steam inside the can becomes just a few drops of water, which take up less space than the steam. There is more room for air in the can, but air can't get inside, so the air pressure inside the can drops. Air pressure on the outside of the can is greater than inside, and the air pushes on the can, crushing it.

Your student should understand that the can was crushed due to greater air pressure outside the can than inside the can. She should understand that the differences in pressure were a result of heating liquid molecules to a gas.

Answers:

1. liquid molecules

2. gas molecules

3. a gas

4. no

5. a liquid

Safety

Never leave your student unattended near a stove, oven, or microwave. Use extreme caution when working with boiling water. Never leave your student unattended near hot or boiling water.

Activity 4. Optional: Make a Barometer *(Offline)*

Instructions

Teaching:

Talk about how air pressure rises and falls. Meteorologists are interested in this because changes in air pressure often mean a change in weather. They use tools such as a barometer to measure air pressure. Farmers and marine workers are also very interested in air pressure. Your student will make a simple barometer to observe air pressure.

What to Expect:

High air pressure will push on the water inside the bottle, forcing water up into the straw. Low air pressure will not push as greatly, and the water level in the straw will fall. The change in air pressure will usually be accompanied by a change in weather, such as rain or storms when the pressure falls.

Answers:

Analysis:

1. Water in the drinking straw will either rise or fall each day.

2. The water may rise and fall in response to weather. Check your student's observations.

3. The water in the straw will drop when air pressure is low and rise when it is high.

Conclusion:

Read your student's conclusion to see that she described using how the water in the barometer rose and fell in response to changes in air pressure.

Learning Coach Guide
Lesson 2. Optional: Forces in Flight

This lesson presents the principles behind an airplane's ability to fly. These forces include lift, thrust, weight, and drag. Your student will learn to describe these forces and demonstrate them in a simple experiment.

Lesson Objectives

- Describe the forces present in flight: lift, weight, thrust, and drag.
- Recognize that density of a solid stays the same even if the object's shape or size changes.

PREPARE

Approximate lesson time is 60 minutes.

Materials

For the Student

    📖 How Does an Airplane Fly?

        household item - spatula

        plastic - container, lg, or bathtub

        paper clip (10)

        paper, notebook - 5 cm x 25cm (2" x 10")

        scissors

        water

        paper, 8 1/2" x 11"

For the Adult

    📖 How Does an Airplane Fly? Answer Key

Lesson Notes

When airplanes fly, four main forces are at work: thrust, drag, lift, and weight. Propellers or jet engines produce a force that results in the plane's moving forward. This force is called *thrust*. Air friction or air resistance works in the direction opposite the thrust. This force is called *drag*. The upward force that makes the plane rise is called *lift*. And the downward force of gravity on the plane is the weight of the plane.

Action, Reaction, and Sir Isaac Newton

Sir Isaac Newton made many important discoveries about forces and gravity. One of his discoveries was that for every action, there is an equal and opposite reaction. This is now known as Newton's Third Law of Motion, and can be demonstrated by a jet engine. When a jet engine is running, the action of the engine pushes hot gases out of the back with a tremendous force. And for every action, according to Newton, there is an equal and opposite reaction. In this case, the opposite action is that the plane goes forward. The greater the thrust backward, the faster the plane moves forward.

Why a Plane Stays Up in the Air

Flying things stay up because they keep pushing something down--usually air. This creates an equal and opposite push up on the plane. If you are under an airplane shortly after it takes off, you will feel a massive wash of air coming straight down.

Airplanes with fixed wings are pushed forward through the air by their engines--this is *thrust*.

- The wing is tilted up at the front, and when air strikes the bottom of the wing it gets pushed down as it follows the slant of the wing. So the wing pushes on the air, making the air go down. This action causes an equal and opposite reaction--the wing gets pushed up.
- Air tries to stick to the top of the wing, too. Even with the wing tilted up at the front, air moving over the top of the wing hangs onto the wing, and unless the wing's tilt is too much, the air tends to move smoothly down over the top of the wing. By the time this air gets to the back of the wing and loses contact with it, the air is being directed downward--pulled down by the top of the wing. As an equal and opposite reaction, the wing gets pulled up at the same time. This turns out to be the source of most of the lift for an airplane.

Keywords and Pronunciation

Daniel Bernoulli (DAHN-yuhl bur-NOOL-ee)

drag : The push that holds an object back as it moves through a gas or liquid. Drag is the opposite force created when the thrust of the engine causes the airplane to meet with air resistance.

lift : The upward force acting on an airfoil. Lift is the force that allows planes to take off and rise into the air.

thrust : A force or push. The engine of an airplane is what causes the force of thrust to occur.

weight : The result of the force of gravity acting on mass. Weight is measured in newtons.

TEACH
Activity 1. Optional: Optional Lesson Instructions (Online)

Activity 2. Optional: The Forces Involved in Flight (Online)
Instructions

Have your student read through the Explore on her own. Reinforce and explain difficult concepts as needed.

Explore Suggestions:

Check your student's understanding by asking these questions:

1. What is the action and opposite reaction involved in airplane thrust? (The action is a plane's engine pushing out fuel gases, and the reaction is the forward movement of the plane.)
2. How is an airplane's wing involved in lifting the airplane up into the air? (The wing's upper and lower surfaces deflect air downward.) Because the wing is pushing the air downward, the wing is pushed upwards by an equal and opposite force--enough to fly!)
3. How do the bottom and top of the wing cause air to go downward? The bottom of the wing deflects the air downward. The air flowing over the top of the wing likes to stay close to the wing, and usually flows nicely along the wing surface. Because of the wing's shape and tilt, this means that air also travels toward the ground as it leaves the wing.

Note:

This explanation is NOT the one you will usually find in popular descriptions of flight. Most of those descriptions refer to an important principle--called the Bernoulli principle--of how fluids and pressures work. Most of those explanations make a mistake in applying the Bernoulli principle, however, and give a simple but incorrect explanation that insists a wing has to be longer over the top than over the bottom. This explanation, however, does not explain how airplanes can fly upside down. The simple explanation given here helps provide intuitive explanations--it doesn't really matter whether the distance over the top or bottom of the wing is longer, as long as the wing is able to push enough air downward to generate the required force upward.

After this activity, check to see if your student can:

- Describe the forces present in flight: lift, weight, thrust, and drag.

If your student has difficulty with any of these concepts, you may wish to review the Explore with her and have her explain the key points on each screen.

Activity 3. Optional: How Does an Airplane Wing Work? *(Offline)*
Instructions
Teaching:

Your student may have difficulty understanding the way air flow pushes up on a surface like a wing. This activity is a simple way to demonstrate this concept. Review how wings work--they push a lot of air downward as they move through the air. The bottom of the wing just deflects air downward. The air going over the top of the wing stays close to the wing and gets pulled along the top surface. By the time the air leaves the back of the wing, it is traveling downward. For the illustration and labeling page, allow your student to look back at the illustrations in the Explore section.

What to Expect:

Your student should notice that the tilted spatula is pushed up by the force of the water, similar to how an airplane wing is pushed up by the air. When your student blows on the strip of paper, the paper will rise because the moving air is trying to stay close to the top of the paper, so the paper actually lifts up. Your student should understand that these two factors are what create lift for an airplane.

Safety
If you use a bathtub instead of a large container, do not leave your student unattended while the bathtub is full of water.

Activity 4. Optional: Paper Airplanes *(Online)*
Instructions
Encourage your student to take advantage of this fun way to investigate flight. The website provides interesting airplane patterns for your child to try. It also has fascinating background information about Ken Blackburn's record-breaking feats. This is a natural and simple way for children to explore a scientific principle that can seem very complex.

Safety
As usual, you may wish to preview any books or websites listed in this lesson.

Name _____   Date _____

How Does an Airplane Fly? Answer Key

Airplanes can weigh nearly 200 tons, so how do they ever get off the ground? Keep in mind that:

- Rushing air hits the bottom of the wing and pushes it up while being deflected downward.
- Air also travels over the top of the wing. It follows the top surface smoothly all the way to the back of the wing, and the shape of the wing causes this air to move downward off the back of the wing.
- All this air pulled downward by the wing, causes the wing to be pulled upward.

You can demonstrate both ways that a wing is lifted up.

Materials
notebook paper, 5 cm x 25 cm (2 in x 10 in) strip
book
paper clips (10)
scissors
kitchen utensil – spatula
water
container, large, or bathtub

Demonstrate that rushing air hits the bottom of the wing and pushes it up.
1. Fill a bathtub or very large container with water.
2. Place a spatula underwater and tilt the flat part up a little, like an airplane wing.
3. Push the spatula through the water. You should be able to feel the spatula being pushed up by the water as you move it through.

How Does an Airplane Fly? Answer Key

Demonstrate that rushing air over the top of the wing sticks close to the wing.

1. Cut a strip of paper 5 cm x 25 cm. Hold one end against your chin, below your mouth.
2. Blow over the top of the strip. As the air tries to stay close to the paper, it pulls the paper up. The paper should rise.
3. Attach a paper clip to the end of the strip and repeat steps 2 and 3. Then add more paper clips to see how many you can lift this way.

Just as the air moving over the top of the wing helps keep a plane in the sky, blowing on the paper causes it to rise. The moving air near the top of the paper stays close to the paper, and so gets pulled down by the curved paper. This pull-down on the air (action) is balanced by a pull up on the paper (reaction)—the paper rises up.

1. What happens to the paper when you stop blowing? **The moving air no longer creates the action, so the paper no longer has a reaction.**

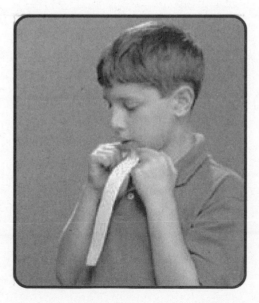 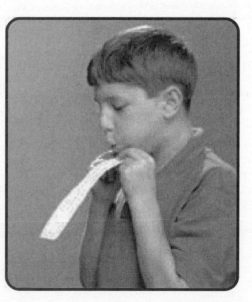

How Does an Airplane Fly? Answer Key

Review the information in the Explore activity. Label the picture of the airplane with the words *lift, thrust, drag,* and *weight.* Illustrate how the air pushes on the bottom and pulls on the top of the wing.

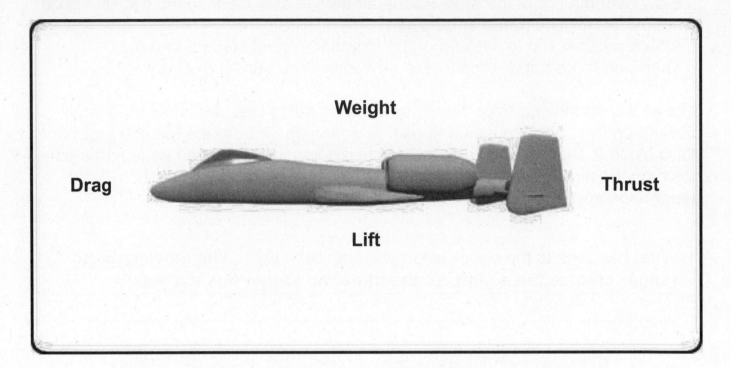

Learning Coach Guide
Lesson 3. Optional: Density

Physical properties of matter include size, shape, color, feel, mass, and volume. Density is another physical property of matter. *Density* describes how much mass is in a certain volume of an object. Your student will calculate density and then compare the densities of some objects. They may be made of the same or different materials as well as differing in shape and size.

Lesson Objectives

- Define *density* as how tightly the matter of an object is packed together.
- Recognize that density of a solid stays the same even if the object's shape or size changes.
- Compare the densities of objects with the same shape and volume.
- Predict whether a substance will sink or float by comparing its density with the density of water.

PREPARE

Approximate lesson time is 60 minutes.

Materials

For the Student

- Air Density

  household item - tape measure

  balloon (2)

  bowl

  water - hot

  water - ice

Lesson Notes

Volume is the amount of space an object takes up. The amount of "stuff" in any object is called *mass*. The ratio between an object's mass and its volume, or size, is the object's *density*.

Objects can be exactly the same size but have different masses. A baseball, for example, is heavier than a plastic foam ball, even when they are the same size. The baseball has more mass--more matter packed into the same amount of space--so its density is also greater.

Density has nothing to do with an object's shape. If you melted a stainless-steel spoon and molded it into any shape, its density would stay the same. If you chopped up the spoon into tiny bits, all the bits would have the same density. And if you melted a bunch of stainless-steel spoons and combined them to make one big stainless-steel spoon, the density of the new spoon would be the same as the density of each the smaller spoons. All the spoons are made of the same material--stainless steel--and the density of the stainless steel stays the same, no matter what shape it takes.

Calculating Density

We calculate density by dividing an object's mass by its volume, and we express the density of an object as *density = mass/volume*.

We measure mass in grams (g), and we measure volume in cubic centimeters (cm³). So we express density in grams per cubic centimeters, or g/cm³.

Keywords and Pronunciation

density : The mass of an object divided by its volume. A baseball has a higher density than a plastic ball of the same size.

mass : The amount of stuff in any object. The mass of an object is the same on Earth as it is on the moon.

volume : The amount of space any object takes up. You can measure the volume of a liquid using a graduated cylinder.

TEACH
Activity 1. Optional: Optional Lesson Instructions (Online)

Activity 2. Optional: Mass Divided by Volume (Online)
Instructions

Have your student read through the Explore on his own. Reinforce and explain difficult concepts as needed.

Explore Suggestions:

If you have a balance, gather some objects of the same size from around the house. Have your student guess which one she thinks has the greatest mass, then use the balance to see if she is correct.

After this activity, check to see if your student can:

- Define *density* as mass per unit volume.
- Calculate an object's density by dividing its mass by its volume.
- Recognize that density of a solid stays the same even if its shape or size changes.

If your student has difficulty with any of these concepts, you may wish to use an alternate explanation, like the following one.

Imagine you have a pile of sand and a stack of small paper cups. You fill each cup to the brim with sand. Would you expect that each filled cup weigh the same? Absolutely! Does each filled cup weigh less than the original pile of sand? Of course! Does each filled cup weigh the same as the other filled cups? They should - after all they are practically identical.

Now imagine that you have a stack of larger juice cups. If you fill them each to the brim with sand, they will again be of equal weight to each other. If you compare a filled larger cup with a filled smaller cup, will they weigh the same? Keep in mind that it is a larger cup filled with the exact same stuff - in this case sand. So you can expect it to weigh *more* than the smaller filled cup.

These examples show an interesting point. The same stuff (sand) seems to weigh different amounts, depending on the container! How can that be? Looks as though weight alone is not a good way to describe a property of sand, or any other substance.

Now imagine you have another container with the same volume as the original small cup, but with a different shape, such as a small square juice carton. Both the small cup and juice carton hold the same amount of sand. When they are both filled with sand, will they weigh the same? Yes! That's because there is the same amount, or volume, of sand in each container, regardless of the shape. Even if two containers have different shapes, if they are the same volume, then anything else we fill the volume with will weigh the same in the two containers.

If one container has *twice* the amount of volume as another, how much more will the stuff we put inside weigh? That's right- twice as much! If we know that one liter of sand weighs 1.8 kilograms, then we know, without weighing it, that 2 liters will weigh 3.6 kilograms and half a liter will weigh 0.9 kilograms

---

This shows that there is a very important connection between the volume of stuff (such as sand) and it's weight. For any substance, there's a number that helps us convert the volume to weight. For our sand example we used the number 1.8 since we knew that the sand weighed 1.8 kilograms for every liter, or 1.8 kg per liter.

This number is known as the *density* of a substance. It is a property of the substance itself, whether you have a small or large amount. No matter how much sand you have, and no matter what the shape or size of the container it is in, it will always have the same density.

Activity 3. Optional: Density and Air Temperature *(Offline)*

Instructions

Teaching:

Review density. Density is the mass per unit volume. Because air is matter, it has density. Remind your student of the Air Bag activity she did in lesson one. Which air was denser, the warm air or cold air? Why?

What to Expect:

The cold balloon will have a smaller circumference than the warm balloon. Cooling the balloon caused its molecules to come together and move in a smaller space, which means there was the same amount of mass in a smaller amount of space. It was packed more tightly.

Answers:

1. Check your student's observations.
2. Gas molecules at lower temperatures move more slowly don't press as hard on the balloon. Gas molecules at higher temperatures move more quickly and push out on the balloon wall, creating more space for themselves.
3. The cold balloon contained denser air.

Learning Coach Guide
Lesson 4. Optional: Buoyancy

Your student will explore the relationship between density and buoyancy. *Buoyancy* is the phenomenon of an object floating. It often involves an object in water. If an object is less dense than water it will float. If it is more dense, it will sink. Investigate the buoyancy of different liquids and the mechanics of submarines.

Lesson Objectives

- Predict whether a substance will sink or float by comparing its density with the density of water.
- Explain Archimedes' observation that the buoyant force of water on an object is equal to the weight of water that the object displaces.
- Define buoyancy as an object's tendency to float.
- Recognize that an object denser than water will sink unless it is shaped so that the total density of the object is less than an equal volume of water.

PREPARE

Approximate lesson time is 60 minutes.

Materials

For the Student

crayons, 64 colors or more - same 4 colors as food coloring

cup, plastic (4)

drinking glass - clear

food coloring - 4 colors

funnel

graduated cylinder

markers - permanent

oil, cooking

rubbing alcohol

spoon

water

🖳 Bottle Submarine

bathtub

bottle, plastic - 500 mL (20 oz.)

clay

tubing, plastic aquarium - 63.5 cm (25 inches)

scissors

tape, clear

washer, metal - (2.5 cm/1 in diameter) (3)

cup, plastic - clear

dimes (10)

golf ball

marbles

table-tennis ball

paper, 8 1/2" x 11"

tape, masking

Lesson Notes

Archimedes was a Greek mathematician and inventor who made many discoveries important to science. One was the water-displacement method of measuring volume. But Archimedes made many other discoveries, including a law of buoyancy, which is now called *Archimedes' Principle*. In simple terms, *buoyancy* is what makes an object float in a fluid. Archimedes' Principle states that an object whose overall density is less than the density of water will float, and an object whose overall density is greater than the density of water will sink. When you compare the weight of two different objects that have the same volume, the denser material *weighs* more, because it has more, or more massive, molecules packed into the same space. And weight and density affect buoyancy. Gravity pulls objects down toward Earth with a constant force, but if you lower an object into water, the water pushes right back on the object. The force of the water on the object is called the *buoyant force*.

If the object is made of a material that is less dense than water, at a certain point the force of the water pushing up will match the force of gravity, or the weight of the object. At that point, the force of gravity matches the force of the water pushing back, and the object will float. If the object is made of material that is denser than water, the force of the water pushing back is less than the force of gravity, and the object will sink.

Archimedes' Principle applies to gases and liquids as well. *Helium*, for example, is a gas that is less dense than air. Because helium is less dense than air, a balloon filled with helium rises.

Keywords and Pronunciation

Archimedes (ahr-kuh-MEE-deez)

Archimedes' Principle : Any body in a fluid is acted upon by a buoyant force equal to the weight of fluid displaced by the body.

buoyancy (BOY-uhnt-see) : the tendency of an object to float

King Hieron (HIY-uh-rahn)

TEACH
Activity 1. Optional: Optional Lesson Instructions *(Online)*

Activity 2. Optional: What Sinks, What Floats? *(Online)*
Instructions

Have your student read through the Explore on her own. Reinforce and explain difficult concepts as needed.

Explore Suggestions:

Check your student's understanding by asking these questions:

1. What is the definition of density? (mass divided by volume)
2. The density of a fresh egg is 1.2 g/mL. The density of a spoiled egg is 0.9 g/mL. How can you find out if an egg is fresh or spoiled? (Put it in water. If it floats it is spoiled.)

After this activity, check to see if your student can:

- Define buoyancy as an object's tendency to float.
- Predict whether a substance will sink or float by comparing its density with the density of water.
- Explain Archimedes' observation that the buoyant force of water on an object is equal to the weight of water that the object displaces.

If your student has difficulty with any of these concepts, you may wish to review the Explore with her and have her explain the key points on each screen.

Activity 3. Optional: Liquid Layers *(Offline)*
Instructions

Teaching:

Review how density is related to buoyancy. The buoyant force of water or air acts opposite to the force of gravity, pushing where gravity pulls down. If an object, such as a rock or air filled balloon, is denser than water or air, the buoyancy force will not keep it afloat and it will sink. Less-dense objects, such as wood or a helium filled balloon, will be held afloat by the buoyant force.

Archimedes' Principle states that an object whose overall density is less than the density of water will float, and an object whose overall density is greater than the density of water will sink. This applies to gases as well. This activity focuses on water.

Troubleshooting:

You may not see a clear separation of the alcohol and water. The blue food coloring will appear darker at the top then fade throughout the two layers. The alcohol is less dense than the water and will be floating on top of the layer of water.

Avoid using the term *weight* when discussing *density*.

What to Expect:

The liquids will arrange themselves into the water in the following manner from top to bottom: alcohol, cooking oil, water, and honey. Your student should understand that the alcohol and cooking oil are less dense than water. The honey is denser. Your student should also understand that the buoyant force of water pushes the less-dense liquids up, but the denser liquids are pulled down harder by gravity.

Activity 4. Optional: Bottle Submarine *(Offline)*

Instructions

Teaching:

If needed, discuss density and buoyancy. Density is the amount of mass a substance has per unit of volume, or space. The *buoyant force* is the force that causes an object to float in a fluid. Archimedes' Principle states that an object whose overall density is less than the density of water will float, and an object whose overall density is greater than the density of water will sink.

Troubleshooting:

You may use a large washtub, basin, or sink instead of a bathtub. As you push the bottle into the water, you may need to hold the clay around the larger hole.

What to Expect:

At first the bottle will float on the water's surface. Next, air bubbles will escape from the holes as you push the bottle down into the water. Finally, when your student blows into the tubing, water will be forced out and replaced by air. The submarine will rise to the surface. Your student should understand that water is denser than air, and if you replace air with water the submarine will sink. It will rise when you replace water with air.

Answers:

Analysis

1. The submarine floated at first because it was full of air. Air is less dense than water so the buoyant force of water kept it afloat.
2. Denser water replaced the air, so it sank.
3. Less dense air replaced the water, so the bottle rose.
4. Submarines rise and sink by alternately taking in air or water.

Activity 5. Optional: The Physics of Underwater Diving *(Offline)*

Instructions

Teaching:

Review density if necessary.

What to Expect:

Eventually your student will tape enough dimes to the table-tennis ball to sink it. The golf ball and marble will not need any dimes to help them sink.

Learning Coach Guide
Lesson 5. Optional: Shape and Buoyancy

Density and the shape of an object determine whether an object will sink or float. This explains why objects that seem to be made of dense materials, such as a steel ocean liner, float. Investigate why overall density is important to principles of buoyancy. Have your student use what she has learned to make an unsinkable boat.

Lesson Objectives

- Recognize that an object denser than water will sink unless it is shaped so that the total density of the object is less than an equal volume of water.
- Identify how the shape of an object affects its ability to float.
- Define pressure as the force exerted on a surface and recognize that pressure is measured in a unit called the pascal.

PREPARE

Approximate lesson time is 60 minutes.

Materials

For the Student

🖳 Unsinkable!

clay
bowl - large
graduated cylinder
spring scale
water

Lesson Notes

Recall that the buoyant force is the force of a fluid pushing up on an object placed in the fluid. As you lower a wood block into water, gravity pulls down on the block and the buoyant force pushes back. Wood is less dense than water, so the upward force of buoyancy balances out the downward force of gravity. When the upward buoyant force is equal to the block's weight, the block floats.

How Shape Affects Buoyancy

An object's shape also has a lot to do with how buoyant the object is. Changing the shape of an object doesn't change the density of the material the object is made of. But changing the shape changes the object's capacity to hold air, which is less dense than liquid.

In a steel-hulled ship, air fills the space inside the hull below the water line, whether the space is open to the air or covered by a deck. And the density of air is much less than the density of water. When enough air fills the space inside the hull below the water line, the overall density of the ship becomes less than the density of water. By *overall density*, we mean the average or mean density of the object, or total mass divided by total volume. What counts here is the overall density of the ship and the air that make up the portion below the water line.

Swim Bladders and Ballast Tanks

For an object to stay at a certain depth in the water without sinking or rising it must have the same overall density as the water at that depth. Fish and submarines can change their buoyancy and remain at a certain depth in the water without effort. Most bony fish change their overall density by regulating the amount of gas in their swim bladders--balloon-like organs that can take in gas from the fish's blood and can also let the gas out.

Submarines have air tanks, called *ballast tanks*, and they work somewhat like a fish's swim bladder. As the tanks fill with water, the sub's overall density increases and the sub dives. To get back to the surface, the crew pumps air back into the tanks and forces out the water. When the sub weighs less than the water, it floats to the surface.

Keywords and Pronunciation

buoyancy (BOY-uhnt-see) : the tendency of an object to float

TEACH
Activity 1. Optional: Optional Lesson Instructions *(Online)*

Activity 2. Optional: How Does Shape Affect Buoyancy? *(Online)*
Instructions
Have your student read through the Explore on his own. Reinforce and explain difficult concepts as needed.

Explore Suggestions:

Check your student's understanding by asking the following questions:

1. Which has a greater overall density: a solid rubber ball or a blown-up rubber raft? (rubber ball)
2. Explain how a swim bladder works to raise or lower a fish as it swims. (The swim bladder inflates and deflates with oxygen in the fish's blood. As the fish swims, its swim bladder expands or contracts allowing the fish to regulate its overall density.)
3. Finish this sentence: If an object is denser than water, it will _____. If an object is shaped so its overall density is less than water, it will _____. (sink, float)

After this activity, check to see if your student can do the following:

- Identify how the shape of an object affects its ability to float.
- Recognize that if an object is denser than water it will sink unless it is shaped so that as it sinks into the water it can displace a weight of water equal to the the weight of the object itself.

If your student has difficulty with any of these concepts, you may wish to review the Explore with her and have her explain the key points on each screen.

Activity 3. Optional: Unsinkable! *(Online)*
Instructions
Teaching:

After your student views the movie about buoyancy and density, discuss the concept of overall density if needed. The difference between the buoyancy of a sinking steel nail and a floating steel boat of the same mass of steel is due to overall density. The shape of the boat allows enough air into its spaces so that its overall (average or mean) density is actually less than the density of water.

When the overall density of an object is less than the density of water, it floats. The force of the object pushing down on the water is balanced by the buoyant force of water pushing up. The mass of the object and the mass of the water it displaces are equal. Had the object displaced less water, it would have sunk.

Troubleshooting:

Work slowly through the activity, and encourage your student to read the entire activity and view the movie as many times as needed. The terms used here may be confusing. Aim for your student to understand that changing the shape of the clay ball to a boat allows air inside, which is less dense than clay. The force of gravity pulling down on the air and clay is not enough to overcome the buoyant force of water pushing up. The clay boat floats.

Assist your student in reading the measurements on the cylinder if needed.

If the mass of the boat and the amount of water displaced are not exactly equal, they should be close. The differences will be due to experimenter error. Have your student repeat the activity to see if her results are different.

What to Expect:

The amount of water displaced by the clay boat should be equal to the mass of the boat. One milliliter of water is equal to one gram of water. The boat should displace an amount of water very near 50 mL.

Your student should understand that the clay boat floats because its overall density is less than that of water. She should also understand that the shape of an object could determine whether or not it will float in water and be able to identify shapes that would most likely float.

Answers:

Observations:

1. 50 mL (or very close)
2. 50 g (or very close)
3. Yes

Conclusions:

1. The object must displace an amount of water, which has a mass equal to the object's mass.
2. The force of gravity pulling the boat down is balanced with the buoyant force of water pushing up.
3. The force of gravity pulling the boat down is greater than the buoyant force of water pushing up.
4. Key features: An inflated Godzilla has less overall density than a deflated Godzilla because its shape allows more air inside. Because it has less overall density, it displaces an amount of water equal to its mass and floats. The deflated Godzilla displaces an amount of water less than its mass and sinks.

Learning Coach Guide
Lesson 6: Unit Review

During this unit your student has learned a lot about Forces in Fluids--from the forces involved in flight and buoyancy to the meaning of *density* and how to apply an understanding of that meaning. Your student will review these concepts and take the unit assessment.

Lesson Objectives

- Explain that atmospheric pressure decreases with height above sea level and water pressure increases with depth below sea level.
- Recognize that an object denser than water will sink unless it is shaped so that the total density of the object is less than an equal volume of water.
- Define pressure as the force exerted on a surface and recognize that pressure is measured in a unit called the pascal.
- Describe the forces present in flight: lift, weight, thrust, and drag.
- Measure the density of a substance or object and predict whether it will sink or float in water.

PREPARE

Approximate lesson time is 60 minutes.

Lesson Notes

Pressure

Atoms and molecules are always in motion. When you blow up a balloon, the air molecules inside the balloon bounce off each other and the inside surface of the balloon. This force of the air molecules pushing on the inside of the balloon is called *air pressure*. But air is also pushing on the outside of the balloon. The air in the Earth's atmosphere pushes on everything, because gravity is always pulling the air molecules down toward Earth.

The pressure of a fluid such as air or water is not the same everywhere on Earth. Air pressure changes with height above sea level. Water pressure also changes, with depth below sea level.

Forces in Flight

Flying airplanes have four main forces at work in them: thrust, weight, drag, and lift. The engines of a jet produce a force that moves the plane forward. This force is called *thrust*. The downward force of gravity on the plane is the plane's *weight*. The upward force that causes the plane to rise is called *lift*. *Drag* tends to slow the plane down.

The shape of a streamlined wing is called an *airfoil*.

When the lift (upward force) is greater than the plane's weight (downward gravitational force) the plane takes off and rises into the air. When the thrust (movement forward) is equal to the drag, the plane keeps moving forward at a constant speed.

Density

An object's mass, divided by its volume, is called its *density*. You can express this as density = mass ÷ volume. Objects that have the same mass can have a very different density, depending on how tightly their molecules are packed together or on the sizes of the various molecules that compose them. A piece of gold and a piece of silver the same size have a different density because the molecules of gold are larger than the molecules of silver.

Buoyancy

The buoyancy of an object in water depends on the object's density. Gold, no matter how large or small a piece of it is, always has the same density (about $20g/cm^3$). Gold will sink in water because it is denser than water, which is $1g/cm^3$.

Shape and Buoyancy

If you change the shape of an object, however, you change its overall density. If you shape a piece of gold into a ship, for example, when you calculate its overall density you must also include the volume of air that is inside the gold ship. Because air is less dense than water, the gold ship's overall density would be less than the density of the gold itself.

TEACH
Activity 1. Optional: Optional Lesson Instructions *(Online)*

Activity 2. Optional: Forces Review *(Online)*
Instructions

Your student will review some of the key concepts presented in this unit along with some of the illustrations and photos used in the lessons. Have her read through the Explore on her own. Reinforce and explain difficult concepts as needed.

After this activity, check to see if your student can do the following:

- Define *pressure* as the force exerted on a surface and recognize that pressure is measured in a unit called the *pascal*.
- Explain that atmospheric pressure decreases with height above sea level while water pressure increases with depth below sea level.
- Describe the forces present in flight, including lift, weight, thrust, and drag.
- Measure the density of a substance or object and predict whether it will sink or float in water.
- Recognize that an object denser than water will sink unless it is shaped so that the total density of the object is less than an equal volume of water.

If your student has difficulty with any of these concepts, you may wish to review the Explore with her and have her explain the key points on each screen.

Activity 3. Optional: Aerodynamic Olympics *(Online)*
Instructions
Teaching:

Allow your student time to review concepts as needed before beginning the review.

What to Expect:

Your student should be able to answer six out of seven questions correctly. If not, she should study concepts she does not understand and then take the review again.

Answer for Question 5:

The boat floats because it shaped so that the amount of water it displaces is less than its weight. The air inside the boat makes the overall density of the boat less.

Activity 4. Optional: ZlugQuest Measurement *(Online)*

Learning Coach Guide
Lesson 1: Working Together

The human body is a miracle of efficiency. Our body systems all keep us alive, from the ones that allow us to move to those that fight disease. Scientists have studied these systems in detail, using specific terms so we can all communicate about them. Let's examine what they have found and see what makes the human body so remarkable.

Various systems in our bodies interact to make them work like smoothly flowing machines. From the nervous system to the immune system, our bodies are able to live for up to a hundred years--sometimes even more. In this lesson, your student will be introduced to the various systems and their functions.

Lesson Objectives

- Identify the various body systems and their functions.
- Define a body system as cells, tissues and organs working together to perform a certain job.
- Describe the five senses and their related sensory organs.

PREPARE

Approximate lesson time is 60 minutes.

Materials

For the Student
- Body Systems Review
- pencil
- Overload!
- timer - stopwatch

For the Adult
- Body Systems Review Answer Key

Lesson Notes

At first glance, the body may seem hopelessly complicated. However, all the pieces fit together in recognizable patterns, or *systems*. This makes understanding the body much simpler. The basic breakdown is this:

- Cells - All living things are made up of cells. Many different kinds of cells come together to form the different parts of human and animal bodies.
- Tissues - Tissues are made up of two or more different kinds of cells.
- Organs - Organs are made up of two or more different kinds of tissues.
- Systems - Systems are made up of different organs.

The Nervous System

The nervous system, which controls the body, has three major parts: the brain, the spinal cord, and the nerves.

Nerve cells that make up a nerve are called *neurons*. These cells transmit electrical signals along their length and across to other neurons. In this way, neurons communicate. Many neurons have endings that allow the organism to sense the outside world. Organs of the nervous system include the eyes, the inner ear, and the brain itself.

The Skeletal System

Bones, made up of different kinds of bone cells, comprise the skeletal system. Bones may feel like rock, but they are actually living tissue. Calcium and phosphorus compounds account for their rigidity. Bones not only support the body, but also protect vital organs such as the brain and heart.

The Muscular System

The muscles comprise the muscular system. We move when muscle cells slide against one another, shortening the muscle fibers and causing the muscle to contract.

- *Voluntary* muscles are under our conscious control. When we wish to grasp an object, the muscles in our hands respond.
- *Involuntary* muscles act without need of conscious control. The heart beats whether one is aware of it or not.

The Respiratory System

The respiratory system gets oxygen into the body and carbon dioxide out. It works with the blood to provide cells with the oxygen they need.

Air passages are made of specialized organs, such as the trachea and the lungs. Air is drawn into the lungs. There it meets air sacs that are lined with blood vessels. Blood then carries the oxygen throughout the body. The respiratory passages also get rid of unwanted gases, particularly carbon dioxide.

The Circulatory System

The circulatory system enables blood to transport life-giving oxygen to cells. It also carries carbon dioxide away from cells to the lungs, where it can be expired. In a similar way, blood:

- Carries hormones from glands
- Carries the food materials cells need to live
- Carries waste away from cells

The central organ of the circulatory systems is the heart. The heart is a pump that sends blood though a series of blood vessels: arteries, veins, and capillaries.

The Endocrine System

The endocrine system makes hormones that control many bodily functions. A *hormone* is a chemical produced in one part of the body that acts on another. Glands produce the hormones that the body uses. The glands that make up the endocrine system include:

- Pineal, hypothalamus, and pituitary, all located in the brain
- Thyroids and parathyroid glands, located in the throat
- Thymus, adrenals, and pancreas, located in the central part of the body

Immune System

The immune system defends against germs, such as viruses, bacteria, protozoa, and fungi.

The skin, along with other external parts, provides one line of protection. Next, the blood contains white blood cells, along with other cells, that attack anything foreign that makes it through. Special chemicals called *antibodies* also attack foreign substances.

Other body systems not treated in this lesson include the digestive, reproductive, and excretory systems.

Keywords and Pronunciation

adrenal (uh-DREE-nl)

cell : The basic unit of all living things.

cytoplasm (SIY-tuh-pla-zuhm)

endocrine (EN-duh-kruhn)

hormone : A chemical produced in one part of the body that acts on cells in another part of the body.

organ : A body part that does a special job within a body system. The heart is the organ that pumps blood through your body.

pancreas (PAN-kree-uhs)

pineal (PIY-nee-uhl)

pituitary (puh-TOO-uh-tair-ee) : A gland found at the base of the brain, responsible for making human growth hormone. The pituitary gland is the main gland responsible for growth.

system : A group of body parts that work together to perform a job. The main body systems are the nervous, skeletal, muscular, endocrine, respiratory, and circulatory systems.

tissue : a group of cells that are similar in structure and that work together to perform a certain function

vertebrae (VUR-tuh-bray)

TEACH

Activity 1: Many Systems, One Body (Online)

Instructions

Have your student read through the Explore on his own. Reinforce and explain difficult concepts as needed.

Explore Suggestions:

Screen 1: On a tissue box, write the word "cells" on each side to remind your student that cells make up tissues. Group a few boxes together to remember that tissues make up organs.

After this activity, check to see if your student can do the following:

- Define a body system as cells, tissues and organs working together to perform a certain job.
- Identify the various body systems and their functions.

If your student has difficulty with any of these concepts, you may wish to review the Explore with him and have him explain the key points on each screen.

Activity 2: Body Systems Review (Offline)

Instructions

Teaching:

Review the levels of organization of body systems. Cells are the building blocks of life and make up tissues. Tissues make up organs, and organs make up systems.

Troubleshooting:

Allow your student to refer back to the Explore section to complete the chart.

Little information is provided on the endocrine system in this lesson. This will be studied in depth later in the unit. A general answer for now is acceptable.

What to Expect:

Your student should be able to identify and describe the functions of the body systems listed in the table. An Answer Key has been provided.

Activity 3: Body Systems Overload (Offline)
Instructions
Teaching:

Your student should be able to do much of this activity independently. If needed, discuss the difference between voluntary and involuntary muscles. Voluntary muscles, such as those used in movement, can be consciously controlled. Involuntary muscles, such as your heart, or the muscles used in digestion, cannot be controlled.

Troubleshooting:

If your student is unable to perform the physical exercises, he may perform a lighter set, such as flexing his feet or arms over and over. Or, have a partner do the exercises and have your student act as "doctor". Have him ask his partner to report how his body systems respond.

What to Expect:

Your student should be able to describe the responses of the body systems studied in this lesson.

Answers:

Observations:

Observations should make sense according to the system being described. For example, your student should not describe the respiratory system response as "my heart beat faster".

1. You cannot feel the response of every body system.
2. You can try to control the response of your skeleton and muscular systems by stopping and starting exercise.
3. Yes, every body system responds during sleep. Breathing slows down and the heart pumps blood more slowly. Your skeleton and muscles relax as your nervous system instructs your body to sleep. Your endocrine system continues to send hormones to other parts of your body.

Safety

This activity involves a few minutes of strenuous physical activity.

ASSESS
Lesson Assessment: Working Together (*Online*)

Students will complete an offline assessment based on the lesson objectives. Print the assessment and have students complete it on their own. Use the answer key to score the assessment, and then enter the results online. The attached answer key is the most current and may not coincide with previously printed guides.

TEACH
Activity 4. Optional: Find Out More: Body Systems (*Online*)
Instructions
Teaching:

Encourage your student to visit these sites if he is interested in exploring the human body.

Troubleshooting:

These sites will have information on the reproductive system.

What to Expect:

Your student will be able to explore several aspects of the various body systems. He can learn how to stay healthy, about injuries and illnesses, and about growing up. He will also read about how the nervous system interacts with other body systems.

Safety

As usual, you may wish to preview the websites listed in this lesson.

Note: The second website suggested in this activity has a reference to the reproductive system.

Body Systems Review Answer Key

Use information from the Explore section to complete the chart.

System Name	Function	Parts	Without this system, I could not...
Nervous	controls the body, giving orders to the rest of the body to carry out	brain, spinal cord, nerves	...do anything! Think, move, feel, speak, hear, taste, etc.
Skeletal and Muscular	supports our bodies and protects our organs, allows movement	bones, muscles, bone cells, muscle cells	...move or stand, and my organs would be unprotected. I also could not lift anything, my heart would not beat, and I could not digest food.
Respiratory	gets oxygen to cells	lungs, blood vessels, air sacs	...breathe in oxygen or get rid of unwanted gases, such as carbon dioxide.
Circulatory	pumps blood to bring oxygen to cells, carries hormones, and carries both food to our cells and waste away from our cells	heart, blood vessels,	...survive. Cells need the blood that is pumped through the body for nourishment, oxygen, and to get rid of cell waste.
Endocrine	makes hormones to control bodily functions	glands, hormones	...send chemical instructions to my body to perform different functions.

Lesson Assessment

Working Together

Answers:

1. Answers may vary, but should include: the respiratory system gets oxygen into the body and provides oxygen to cells.

2. Answers may vary, but should include: the endocrine system makes special chemicals, called hormones, that control bodily functions.

3. Answers may vary, but should include: the nervous system controls the body.

4. Answers may vary, but should include: the circulatory system brings blood and oxygen to cells and carries away cell waste.

5. Answers may vary, but should include: the skeleton and muscular system supports the body, protects organs, and allows movement.

6. The building blocks of life are called **cells**. Two or more of these "building blocks" make up **tissues**. Organs are made from two or more kinds of **tissue**. Two or more organs make up **a system** that performs a certain job.

Learning Coach Guide
Lesson 2: Under Control: Your Nervous System

The nervous system is the control system of the body. It is composed of the brain, brain stem, spinal cord, and the nerves. These all make up an interactive highway of electrical signals by which we sense the world around us and react to it. In this lesson your student will gain an overview of the nervous system and its basic parts.

Lesson Objectives

- Describe the function of the nervous system and identify its parts.
- Describe the five senses and their related sensory organs.
- Compare the voluntary nervous system with the involuntary nervous system.
- Define a reflex as movements that happen very quickly without your thinking about them.
- Explain how neurons carry impulses throughout the body.

PREPARE

Approximate lesson time is 60 minutes.

Materials

For the Student

    📖 Keep Your Brain in Shape

Optional

    coins

    cups

    tape recorder

    toothbrush

Lesson Notes

The Nervous System

Olympian gymnasts are an example of how precise the human nervous system is, and what it can do with proper training. Your student should not think, though, that only athletes have finely tuned nervous systems. Even a seemingly simple act like climbing a flight of stairs is the result of a highly effective system. It is this system that monitors our bodies and the world outside them.

The nervous system receives information not only from the five senses, but through chemical and physical signals inside the body. This information is sent back and forth by means of electrical signals that pass from nerve cell to nerve cell.

The nervous system has three main components:

- Brain - Made of nerves and other tissues, the brain controls almost all body activities, either directly or indirectly.
- Spinal Cord - This is a bundle of nerves that runs down the back of the body and is protected by the vertebrae.
- Nerves - Bundles of nerve cells that are found throughout the body. The brain and the spinal cord are made of nerve cells plus support cells.

The nervous system senses the world in five major ways:

- Seeing
- Hearing
- Smelling
- Touching
- Tasting

Each of these senses is associated with an organ that has specialized nerve cells to do a specific job. Special cells in the eye respond to light, nose cells recognize special chemicals, and the tongue has taste buds to sense flavors.

Voluntary Nervous System

The voluntary nervous system is the part over which we have control. Raising a hand to grasp something is a voluntary movement. We consciously think about raising our hands before they move.

Involuntary Nervous System

The involuntary nervous system is the part over which we have no conscious control. Shivering when you are cold, getting goose bumps, and having a heartbeat are all involuntary.

Animal Nervous Systems

The human nervous system is indeed impressive. It combines voluntary and involuntary parts, the five major senses, and the awareness of internal and external changes. But your student should understand that the nervous systems of all animals, even very basic ones, are extremely successful as well. They simply are attuned to the specific needs of the organism itself.

Keywords and Pronunciation

brain : The control center of the body. The brain tells your body what to do.

nerve : Bundles of axons that are found throughout the body. There are many nerves in hands.

reflex : A movement that happens very quickly, without your thinking about it. When you touch something hot, your hand pulls away quickly in a reflex action.

spinal cord : A thick bundle of nerves that runs up and down the inside of the spine, or backbone. The spinal cord is located inside the backbone.

vertebrae (VUR-tuh-bray)

TEACH
Activity 1: Structure of the Nervous System *(Online)*

Instructions

Have your student read through the Explore on his own. Reinforce and explain difficult concepts as needed.

Explore Suggestions:

Screen 5: Have your student examine the difference between the voluntary and involuntary parts of his body. If he rests very quietly, can he stop his heart? How long can he go without blinking?

After this activity, check to see if your student can:

- Describe the function of the nervous system and identify its parts.
- Describe the five senses and their related sensory organs.
- Compare the voluntary nervous system to the involuntary nervous system.
- Define *reflexes* as movements that happen very quickly, without your thinking about them.

If your student has difficulty with any of these concepts, you may wish to review the Explore with him and have him explain the key points on each screen.

Activity 2: Keep Your Brain in Shape *(Offline)*

Instructions

Teaching:

Your student may try one or all of the brain exercises. You can try them together. Discuss them and the *What's going on?* following each exercise. Discuss how senses (touch, sound, sight, taste, smell) are related to the nervous system.

What to Expect:

Your student should notice some difficulty when he first tries the brain exercises. With time, as the brain makes new connections, they should become easier. Encourage your student to look for ways to train his brain.

ASSESS

Lesson Assessment: Under Control: Your Nervous System *(Offline)*

Students will complete an offline assessment based on the lesson objectives. Print the assessment and have students complete it on their own. Use the answer key to score the assessment, and then enter the results online. The attached answer key is the most current and may not coincide with previously printed guides.

Name _____   Date _____

Nervous System Assessment Answer Key

1. Why is the nervous system sometimes called the *control center*?
   The nervous system controls all functions of the body. It is
   responsible for reflexes, for using senses to understand the outside
   world, for movement, and for thought.

2. Draw a line to match the sense to its sensory organ.

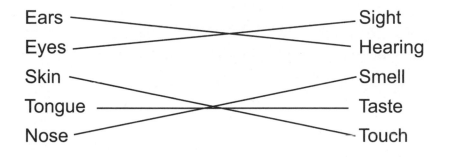

   Ears ——————————————— Sight
   Eyes ——————————————— Hearing
   Skin ——————————————— Smell
   Tongue ————————————— Taste
   Nose ——————————————— Touch

3. Label the picture of the nervous system with the following parts:

   Brain

   Spinal Cord

   Nerves

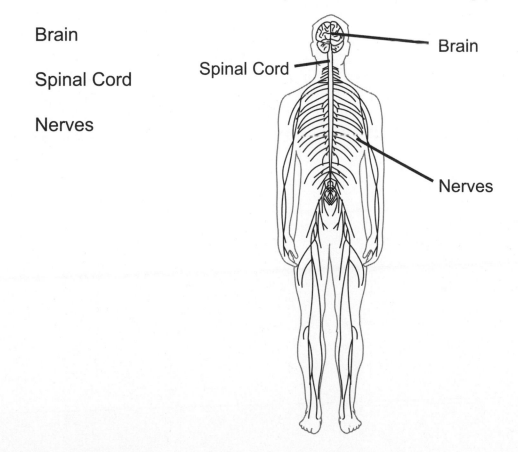

Spinal Cord

Brain

Nerves

Nervous System Assessment Answer Key

4. Which is a reflex--shivering or running? Explain why. <u>Shivering</u>
   is a reflex. A reflex does not require thought from your brain to happen.
   Running requires thinking about moving your legs, seeing where you are
   going, and deciding when to start, stop, go faster, or go slower.

5. What is the difference between your voluntary nervous system
   and your involuntary nervous system? Give an example of each.
   The voluntary nervous system involves things you can control, such
   as deciding when to move a leg, then controlling the movement. The
   involuntary nervous system cannot be controlled. This involves actions
   such as sneezing, getting goose bumps, or other reflexes.

Learning Coach Guide
Lesson 3: Nerves

In this lesson your student will learn about how nerves work and about the structure of the nerve cell. Nerve signals, in the form of electrical impulses, are sent from remote nerves to the spinal cord. The spinal cord often then sends the information to the brain and back again. All of these signals move almost effortlessly to create a smoothly working system.

Lesson Objectives

- Explain how neurons carry impulses throughout the body.
- Identify the parts of a neuron and their functions.
- Name the three main parts of the brain: the cerebrum, cerebellum and brain stem.

PREPARE

Approximate lesson time is 60 minutes.

Advance Preparation

- If you don't already have it, you will need pipe cleaners (five different colors) for the Model Neuron experiment.

Materials

For the Student

- Model Neuron
  pipe cleaners - five different colors
  scissors

Lesson Notes

The nervous system allows us to monitor, and react to, both our internal and external worlds. An example of monitoring the internal world might be the awareness that one is hungry. An example of reacting to the external world might be smelling bacon and walking toward it.

The basis for the nervous system is the nerve cell, or the *neuron*. A typical neuron has three parts:

- Cell body--This is the central part of the neuron and contains the nucleus.
- Dendrites--These branch-like extensions carry nerve signals *toward* the cell body. There are usually many dendrites per cell.
- Axon--This carries nerve signals *away from* the cell body. Most neurons have has one axon.

A nerve impulse from a nearby cell stimulates a dendrite. The nerve signal goes down the dendrite to the cell body. From there it may or may not head down the axon, away from the cell.The cell body can act as a switch. A nerve signal is called an *impulse*. Although the idea that the body uses electricity may seem strange to your student, an impulse is, in fact, an kind of electrical signal. He should understand that "electrical" does not always mean wires and wall sockets. It may help to think of what happens in a neuron in terms of how charged particles move back and forth.

1. An axon that is not carrying a signal has both positively and negatively charged electrical particles. The positively charged particles are on the *outside* of an axon's membrane. The negatively charged particles are on the *inside* of its membrane.

2. When a neuron is stimulated and the signal reaches the axon, some of the positively charged particles change place with the negatively charged particles. This reversal of electrical charge is the signal or impulse.

3. As the signal passes down the axon, the positive and negative particles go back to their original positions. The electrical signal has moved down the axon. This all happens in a few thousandths of a second.

Nerve signals need to travel from one nerve to another, or communication between them would be impossible. There is a graphic in the lesson showing how this happens. In short, the tip of one nerve cell's axon lies next to the dendrite of another. This gap between them is called a *synapse*.

1. When the nerve signal reaches the end of the axon, it causes the cell to release packets of chemicals called *neurotransmitters*.

2. The neurotransmitters cross the synapse and arrive at the dendrite of the next neuron.

3. The arrival of the chemicals causes the formation a new electrical signal in the dendrite.

4. Other chemicals floating in the synapse remove the used neurotransmitters that just transferred the impulse.

Keywords and Pronunciation

axon : The long arm of a neuron that is responsible for conducting nerve impulses away from the cell body.

cell body : The central part of a neuron that contains the nucleus of the cell.

dendrite (DEN-driyt) : The tree-like, branching arms of a neuron, which usually conduct nerve impulses toward the body of the neuron.

glial (GLEE-uhl)

neuron : A nerve cell made up of three main parts: dendrites, a cell body and an axon.

synapse (SIH-naps)

TEACH

Activity 1: Impulse! *(Online)*

Instructions

Have your student read through the Explore on his own. Reinforce and explain difficult concepts as needed.

Explore Suggestions:

Screen 4: Gather friends or siblings together and model how an electrical signal travels through neurons.

Assign a role to each person: cell body, axon, dendrite, and electrical signal.

Check your student's understanding by asking the following questions:

1. Name the parts of a nerve cell. (cell body, axon, dendrite, synapse, and neurotransmitters)

2. Describe how an impulse travels from neuron to neuron. (An electrical signal travels down the axon away from the cell body. At the end of the axon, packets of chemicals called *neurotransmitters* are released and stimulate the dendrite of the next neuron. Dendrites of the next neuron initiate a new electrical signal and pass it to the cell body.)

After this activity, check to see if your student can:

*   Explain how neurons carry impulses throughout the body.
*   Identify the parts of a neuron and their functions.

If your student has difficulty with any of these concepts, you may wish to review the Explore with him and have him explain the key points on each screen.

Activity 2: Model Neuron *(Offline)*
Instructions
Teaching:

During this activity, your student will review the functions of parts of neurons. Using the Explore text, he should be able to do this independently.

Troubleshooting:

Refer to the illustrations when making the model neuron if your student has any trouble.

What to Expect:

Your student will make a model of a neuron he can use to study and review parts of a neuron. He should be able to identify each part and describe its function as well as how neurons carry impulses throughout the body.

Answers:

1. Cell body: the central part of the neuron that contains the nucleus

    Axon: carries nerve signals away from the body.

    Dendrites: carry nerve signals toward the cell body.

    Fatty sheath: covers the axon and allows electrical impulses to "hop" smoothly from place to place.

    Synaptic terminal: emits chemicals called neurotransmitters into synapses, or space between neurons.

2. 1, 2, 5, 4, 3

ASSESS

Lesson Assessment: Nerves (*Offline*)

Students will complete an offline assessment based on the lesson objectives. Print the assessment and have students complete it on their own. Use the answer key to score the assessment, and then enter the results online. The attached answer key is the most current and may not coincide with previously printed guides.

Name _____   Date _____

Nerves Assessment Answer Key

1. Label the cell body, axon, and dendrites on the illustration.

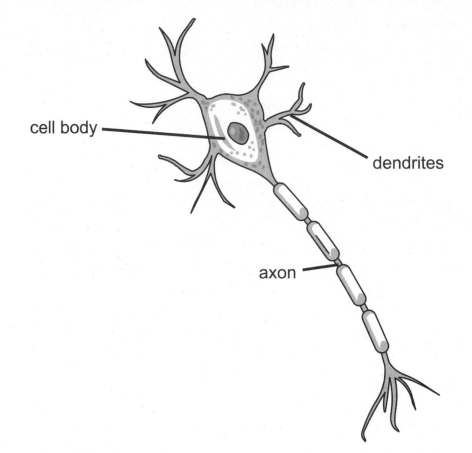

cell body

dendrites

axon

2. Write the job of each part of a neuron in sending impulses from nerve cell to nerve cell.

axon **This carries signals away from the cell body.**

_____

dendrite **This receives signals from neurotransmitters and**
         sends them to the cell body.

cell body **This receives the signal from the dendrites and may**
          pass the signal along to the axon.

Learning Coach Guide
Lesson 4: The Cerebrum, Cerebellum, and Brain Stem

The brain is divided into three major parts. They are the *cerebellum*, *cerebrum*, and *brain stem*. These parts are responsible for all bodily functions, such as movement, memory, and responses to sensation. Your student will make a model to review the parts of the brain. The student will also investigate the *homunculus*, which is a representation of sense receptors in the body.

Lesson Objectives

- Name the three main parts of the brain: the cerebrum, cerebellum and brain stem.

PREPARE

Approximate lesson time is 60 minutes.

Advance Preparation

- You will need instant potato flakes for this science activity.

Materials

For the Student

    📑 Graph Paper

    📑 Map the Homunculus

      ruler, metric

      toothpicks (2)

      food - instant potatoes (360 ml)

      sand - 2 cups (480 ml)

      bags, zipper-close - gallon size

      water - hot, 2.5 cups (600 ml)

For the Adult

    📑 Map the Homunculus Answer Key

Lesson Notes

The brain contains over 100 million neurons and over 5 trillion glial cells to nurture and protect them. It is in control of every action we take all day, from running to tooth brushing. It is responsible for every sensation we have, from feeling the pleasant warmth of the afternoon sun to the talking animals seen in a dream. It also is responsible for a host of activities we aren't aware of, such as maintaining body temperature.

Discuss with your student how it is hard to overstate the brain's complexity or its power. That an organ weighing only 1.5 kilograms has, in a sense, written *Hamlet*, danced in ballets and figured out how to take itself to the moon is nothing short of astonishing.

The brain has three major parts: the cerebrum, the brain stem, and the cerebellum.

The Cerebrum

The cerebrum is the large part of the brain and fills the area nearest the skull. It is the "thinking" part of the brain. The skills of reading, writing, and higher-order thinking are found here.

The outer layer of the cerebrum is the cerebral cortex. It folds in and out, creating a wavy surface for the brain. The cerebrum, with its cerebral cortex, is divided into two halves. Each half is called a *hemisphere*. The hemispheres are connected by a thick bundle of nerves called the *corpus callosum*.

Functions controlled by the cerebrum include memory, problem solving, voluntary muscle control, math skills, speech and musical ability.

The Brain Stem

The brain stem connects the spinal cord to the brain, and is in charge of heart rate, breathing, and other basic bodily functions. The brain stem connects the spinal cord and its densely packed nerves to the brain.

The Cerebellum

The cerebellum controls balance and position and keeps the skeletal muscles coordinated. It is located in the back of the brain, tucked under the tissues of the cerebrum.

The Homunculus

A homunculus is a sensory map of the body, showing us which areas have the largest amounts of sensory neurons. Areas packed with nerve endings, such as the tongue, are represented as particularly large. While the image of the homunculus will make your student laugh--by no means a bad thing--your student should also understand what this map shows us about the brain and the body.

Keywords and Pronunciation

cerebellum (sehr-uh-BEH-luhm)

cerebral (suh-REE-bruhl)

cerebrum (suh-REE-bruhm)

corpus callosum (KOR-puhs ka-LOH-suhm)

glial (GLEE-uhl)

homunculus (hoh-MUHN-kyuh-luhs) : A sensory map of the body.

occipital (ahk-SIH-puh-tl)

parietal (puh-RIY-uh-tl)

temporal (TEM-pruhl)

TEACH

Activity 1: The Thinking Brain *(Online)*

Instructions

Have your student read through the Explore on his own. Reinforce and explain difficult concepts as needed.

Explore Suggestions:

Screen 4: Certain skills and abilities are, in a general sense, assigned to different hemispheres of the brain, as listed here. There are tests available that suggest whether the control of certain activities is centered in the left or right side of your brain.

LEFT BRAIN

logical

sequential

rational

analytical

objective

parts-oriented

RIGHT BRAIN

random

intuitive

holistic

synthetic

subjective

wholes-oriented

After this activity, check to see if your student can:

- Describe some of the main functions of the cerebral cortex, such as movement, memory, and speech.

If your student has difficulty with any of these concepts, you may wish to review the Explore with him and have him explain the key points on each screen.

Activity 2: Map the Homunculus *(Online)*

Instructions

Teaching:

Your student will need your assistance for this activity. The cerebral cortex is the area of the brain responsible for movement, memory, and speech. The sense of touch is controlled here, as well. The homunculus is a representation of how sense receptors are distributed through the body. It does not represent a real person. The hands, lips, and face are large on the homunculus because there are more sense receptors in those areas than in others, such as elbows or knees. Explain to your student that by mapping the homunculus, he will be investigating the connection between sense receptors in his skin and the cerebral cortex.

There is an online calculator provided. If you have one of your own, however, use it to keep the activity completely offline.

What to Expect:

Your student should be able to discriminate between two points and one point of contact when touched with the toothpicks. He should be able to measure the distance between the toothpicks when appropriate. He will need assistance calculating the "Size on Graph Paper" measurement.

Answers:

See answer key. The data in the table is a sample only.

Activity 3: Model Brain *(Offline)*

Instructions

Teaching:

Discuss physical characteristics of the brain such as size (about 1.5 kg), consistency (soft), and color (white and gray).

What to Expect:

Your student will have a model of a brain that is the same size and consistency of a real brain.

ASSESS

Lesson Assessment: The Cerebrum, Cerebellum, and Brain Stem *(Offline)*

Students will complete an offline assessment based on the lesson objectives. Print the assessment and have students complete it on their own. Use the answer key to score the assessment, and then enter the results online. The attached answer key is the most current and may not coincide with previously printed guides.

Name _____   Date _____

Map the Homunculus – Answer Key

The odd-looking homunculus helps us understand how sense receptors are distributed in the body. Each body part is drawn based on the number of sense receptors found there, not on its size. That's why the hands, tongue, and lips are very large and the forehead and knees are not. You can perform a simple touch test to see if the homunculus describes sense receptors in your body.

Materials:
two toothpicks
graph paper
ruler
calculator

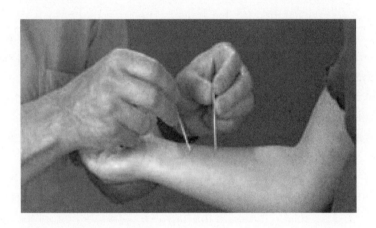

Procedure:
To do the test, you will need a partner.
1. As you look away, have your partner gently touch two toothpicks to the skin of your right forearm as shown. Make sure both toothpicks touch your arm at the same time.
2. You should feel two points of contact. If not, have your partner move the toothpicks farther apart until you do.
3. Lift and move the toothpicks closer together, about 0.5 cm at a time, until you no longer can tell there are two toothpicks touching you. Instead, it should feel like just one toothpick. This means both toothpicks touching your arm are being sensed by the same touch receptor.
4. Measure and record the distance between the two toothpicks and record it in the table. Round to the nearest tenth of a centimeter.
5. Repeat steps one through four on the right side of your body for the other parts listed.

Map the Homunculus – Answer Key

Body Part – RIGHT side	Distance between toothpicks in cm	Size on graph paper
forehead	1.9	
cheek	1.6	
lips	0.3	
nose	0.9	
upper arm	16.3	
lower arm	4.6	
palm	0.5	
elbow	2.0	
fingertips	0.3	
shoulder	4.2	
kneecap	5.0	
calf	8.9	
sole	3.3	
toes	2.6	

Analysis:
1. Be sure to have a calculator nearby to get ready to draw the homunculus. If you do not have one, an online calculator has been provided for you.
2. The closer the receptors are in your tests, the larger they will need to be on the homunculus. You need to find what's called an "inverse" to figure out just how large the part should be.
3. Divide all of your measurements into the number 1.
   Example: Distance = 0.2; 1 ÷ 0.2 = 5. This means this body part will be as large as 5 boxes on graph paper.

Map the Homunculus – Answer Key

4. Write your answer in the "Size on Graph Paper" column.
5. Repeat steps two through four for all measurements.
6. Use the measurements in the "Size on Graph Paper" column to draw a picture of your homunculus on graph paper. Do the best you can to make a normal body shape!

Conclusions:

1. Which part of the brain is responsible for interpreting touch? ___
   Parietal lobe

2. Which side of your body did you test? **right**
   Which side of the brain's sensory cortex did you map? Explain.
   You mapped the left side. Messages from the right side of the
   body are directed to the left side of the brain.

3. How does your homunculus compare to the one you saw in the lesson? _____
   Accept reasonable answers. They should be fairly close.

Interesting fact:
Animals have a homunculus! (Since the Latin word for person is "homo," perhaps an animal would have an "animunculus.") Think about how the homunculus might look for rats, rabbits, or giraffes. How might a giraffe homunculus look if there are a small amount of sensory receptors in its neck?

Name _____   Date _____

Cerebrum Assessment Answer Key

Below is a diagram of how the brain is organized. Fill in the names of the three main parts of the brain and describe their functions.

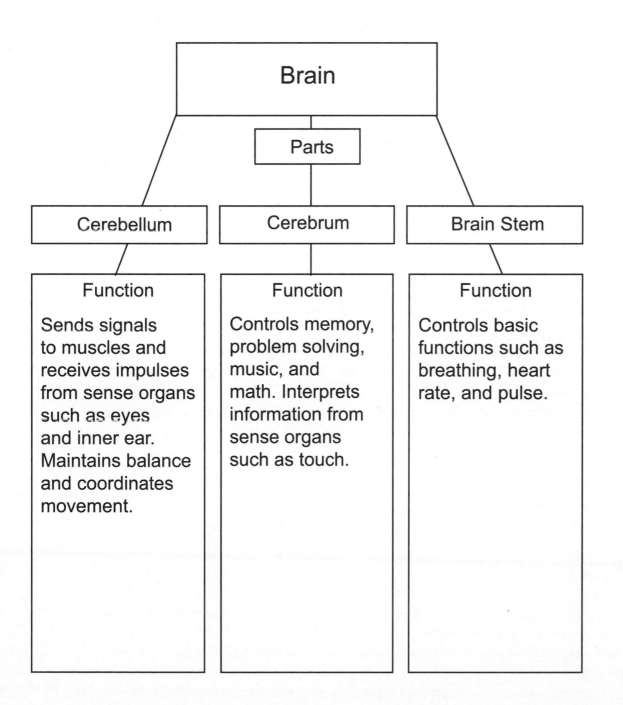

Brain

Parts

Cerebellum	Cerebrum	Brain Stem
Function	**Function**	**Function**
Sends signals to muscles and receives impulses from sense organs such as eyes and inner ear. Maintains balance and coordinates movement.	Controls memory, problem solving, music, and math. Interprets information from sense organs such as touch.	Controls basic functions such as breathing, heart rate, and pulse.

Learning Coach Guide
Lesson 5. Optional: More About the Brain / Other Brain Structures

Learn more about other brain structures such as the *medulla oblongata*, *pons*, and *thalamus*. Explore techniques and equipment used to study the brain. Compare the brains of humans with those of other vertebrates. Attempt everyday tasks with a twist to study the effects of confusing the brain.

Lesson Objectives

- Identify the locations and describe some of the main functions of the cerebellum, brain stem, and the cerebrum.

PREPARE

Approximate lesson time is 60 minutes.

Materials

For the Student

⌨ Brain Tricks

blindfold

household item - pillow

markers

Lesson Notes

The brain is made up of over 100 million neurons, and at least a billion more are in the spinal cord. These critical neurons need protection.

Their primary protection is the skull. The skull is not a single bone but a series of interlocked bony plates. Neurons in the brain are also protected by a series of sheaths that cover the brain and spinal cord. These layers are called the *meninges*.

The brain consists of three major parts. One part, called the *cerebrum*, is necessary for activities such as:

- Reading
- Writing
- Reasoning
- Complex mathematical activities

The *cerebellum* and *brain stem* are the control centers for such functions as:

- Breathing
- Heartbeat rate
- Pupil dilation
- Balance

The brain stem is also connected to a series of brain parts known as the *limbic system*. This is where emotions such as fear and anxiety come from.

There are various techniques for examining the living brain in action to learn how it operates. In one experiment, scientists placed electrical monitors on a person's skull. The person was then shown pictures of different faces. The monitors picked up heightened activity in a particular place in the brain. In this way they determined the area of the brain that is responsible for facial recognition.

A comparison of human brains with those of two other animals, frogs and birds, shows that there are distinct differences.

- Frog--The brain stem and the cerebellum are much larger than the relatively small cerebrum.
- Bird--The cerebellum and the cerebrum are about the same size.
- Human--The cerebrum is largest of all.

The lesson concludes with optical illusions. Optical illusions occur when the brain sees something that is not actually there. They also take place when the brain incorrectly interprets what it sees.

Keywords and Pronunciation

cerebellum (sehr-uh-BEH-luhm)

cerebral (suh-REE-bruhl)

cerebrum (suh-REE-bruhm)

medulla oblongata (muh-DUH-luh ah-blahng-GAH-tuh) : The part of the brain that sends signals between the left and right sides of the brain in vertebrates. The medulla oblongata contains areas that control breathing.

meninges (muh-NIN-jeez) : A membrane that surrounds the brain and spinal cord in vertebrates. The brain surgeon had to cut through the meninges to get to the brain.

pons : Nerve fibers that link the medulla oblongata and cerebellum to the upper parts of the brain. The pons contains areas that receive sensory information from the face.

thalamus (THA-luh-muhs) : The part of the brain that sends signals to the cerebral cortex. The thalamus is located in the lower part of the brain.

TEACH
Activity 1. Optional: Optional Lesson Instructions (Online)

Activity 2. Optional: Brainstorming (Online)
Instructions

Have your student read through the Explore on his own. Reinforce and explain difficult concepts as needed.
Explore Suggestions:

Screen 2: Our brains are protected by bone, skin, and tissue. Use this as an opportunity to discuss why it is important to protect our heads with helmets during activities that might cause injury, such as bike riding or rollerblading.

Check your student's understanding by asking the following questions:

1. Which activities are part of "new brain" activities? Which are part of "old brain" activities? (New: reading, writing, reasoning, complex math activities. Old: breathing, heart rate)

2. How can we study the brain without being able to look directly at it? (Special tests and equipment help us study the brain. Examples: tests in which electrical impulses can be monitored from outside the skull and CAT scans in which certain areas of the brain respond to radiation and show up as different colors on a screen)

After this activity, check to see if your student can:

- Identify the location and describe some of the main functions of the cerebellum, brain stem, and cerebrum.

If your student has difficulty with any of these concepts, you may wish to review the Explore with him and have him explain the key points on each screen.

Safety

As usual, you may wish to preview the websites suggested in this lesson.

Activity 3. Optional: Brain Tricks *(Offline)*

Instructions

Teaching:

The purpose of this activity is to give your student experience and understanding in more tasks involving the brain. By performing these brain tricks, your student will observe how difficult it is for the brain to "unlearn" basic skills or adjust to simple tasks such as balancing. Discuss what brain structures are involved in each task.

Troubleshooting:

You will need to help your student complete test number two. Read the instructions aloud to him.

What to Expect:

Your student will have different degrees of difficulty with each test. He should be able to understand what brain structures or processes are involved in carrying out each task and how each task "confuses" these structures or processes.

Extension:

Have your student visit the Brain Game link in the Resources section for more brain activities including an online interactive test of color and reading memory.

Learning Coach Guide
Lesson 6: Spinal Cord and Nerves

If the brain is the control center of the body, then the spinal cord is its superhighway. It is the central pathway for nerves to get to and from the brain. Many lateral nerves branch off of the spinal cord and go to all parts of the body.

Lesson Objectives

- State that the spine protects the spinal cord.
- Describe how the spinal cord helps in transmitting messages to and from the brain.
- Describe how a nerve signal is transmitted through a reflex arc.

PREPARE

Approximate lesson time is 60 minutes.

Materials

For the Student

💻 Explore your Reflexes

cotton balls

chair

safety goggles

💻 Reaction Ruler

ruler

ruler, metric - meter stick

Lesson Notes

All humans are *vertebrates*. This means we have backbones, as opposed to, say, jellyfish, which have none. The backbone is composed of a series of bones called *vertebrae*.

Inside the backbone is the *spinal cord*. The spinal cord is a large bundle of nerve fibers that runs the entire length of the back.

The spinal cord is critical to the life of any vertebrate organism. If the spinal cord becomes damaged, the brain may be unable to send signals to various parts of the body. Thanks to the advances of modern medical science, many people with spinal cord injuries are able to continue living their lives, though with serious limitations. Before the modern age, however, people rarely survived significant damage to the spinal cord. Because of the spinal cord's great significance, it is not surprising to find that it is defended in several ways. These include:

- The backbone itself, which encases the spinal cord.
- The *meninges*, three layers of protective cushioning that enfold the spinal cord.
- The *cerebro-spinal fluid*, a protective liquid that bathes the spinal cord.

Thirty-one pairs of nerves, called the *spinal nerves*, leave the bony encasement of the backbone and go to all parts of the body. These nerves continue to branch, making contact with the entire surface of the body and all internal organs. Spinal nerves branch out from the spinal cord in a recognizable pattern. Two nerves emerge from any one place in the spinal cord. One goes to the left half of the body and one to the right.

Each spinal nerve attaches to the spine at two locations: a *dorsal* spot (towards the back) and a *ventral* spot (towards the stomach). The dorsal part carries messages from nerve endings *to* the spinal cord. The ventral part carries messages *from* the spinal cord to muscles.

When one touches an object:

- Touch sensors in the fingers are stimulated.
- An electrical signal travels from those nerve endings to a lateral nerve.
- The signal enters the spinal cord by way of the dorsal connection.
- It travels up the spinal cord to the brain stem, where it is routed to the correct part of the brain.

Only then is the conscious mind aware of the object.

Similarly, when one decides to pick up the object:

- The brain sends signals down the spinal cord.
- When those signals reach the correct spinal nerve, they leave the spinal cord by way of the ventral connection.
- The signals travel down your arm into your hand, telling the muscles to contract.

When touching harmful objects, such as a hot surface, there is no time for conscious reflection. The body instead employs a *reflex arc*, which takes place without involvement of the brain. After the nerve signal enters the spinal cord, instead of traveling to the brain stem, it moves in an arc around the spinal cord and leaves by way of the ventral connection.

Keywords and Pronunciation

cerebrospinal (suh-ree-broh-SPIY-nl)

dorsal : Towards the back. A shark's dorsal fin can be seen sticking out of the water when the shark is swimming near the surface.

lateral nerves : Nerves that branch out from the spinal cord, containing many more branches to reach every nerve receptor in the body. Sometimes, as in the disease shingles, a single lateral nerve will become infected with a virus.

meninges (muh-NIN-jeez) : A membrane that surrounds the brain and spinal cord in vertebrates. The brain surgeon had to cut through the meninges to get to the brain.

reflex : Movements that happen very quickly without your thinking about them. Pulling your hand back after touching a hot stove is a reflex action.

ventral : To the front. The man on the beach was lying on his ventral side--on his stomach; the sun was therefore striking his dorsal side warming up his back.

vertebrae (VUR-tuh-bray)

vertebrate (VUR-tuh-bruht) : An animal with a backbone. Mammals, fish, and birds are classified as vertebrates because they have a backbone.

TEACH
Activity 1: Functions of the Spinal Cord *(Online)*

Instructions

Have your student read through the Explore on his own. Reinforce and explain difficult concepts as needed.

Explore Suggestions:

Screen 1: Try this to help your student understand the structure of the spinal cord. Use Cheerios to represent vertebrae. String them on to yarn, representing the spinal cord.

Screen 3: Help your student keep new terms straight by taping a note that says "dorsal" to his back and a note that says "ventral" to his front. You can also practice pointing out dorsal and ventral "sides" on dolls, action figures, pets, and the like.

After this activity, check to see if your student can do the following:

- State that the spine protects the spinal cord.
- Describe how the spinal cord helps in transmitting messages to and from the brain.
- Describe how a nerve signal is transmitted through a reflex arc.

If your student has difficulty with any of these concepts, you may wish to review the Explore with him and have him explain the key points on each screen.

Activity 2: Reflex Exploration *(Offline)*

Instructions

Teaching:

Your student will need your assistance to complete the activity. He may already be aware of reflexes in the human body. Doctors often test the *knee-jerk reflex* and the *plantar reflex*. The plantar reflex is tested by drawing the handle of a special hammer across the sole of the foot. The doctor begins at the heel and moves up toward the big toe. Usually, toes will flex and move together in response. Discuss these and other reflexes, such as the constricting of pupils in bright light.

Explain that reflexes help protect the body from serious injury. Some reflexes, such as breathing, blood pressure, and heart rate adjustments, happen without our being aware of them.

Troubleshooting:

You may need to try the knee-jerk reflex several times before getting it right.

What to Expect:

Your student should observe and experience two examples of reflexes. He should be able to describe the order of signals and responses in a reflex arc.

Answers:

5, 4, 2, 3, 1

Activity 3: Reaction Ruler *(Offline)*

Instructions

Teaching:

Your student will need your assistance to complete the activity. Discuss the different paths certain reactions take. Messages sent in the case of a reflex arc do not go to the brain before being carried out. Other messages must travel to the brain where they are interpreted before a decision is made. Then another message is sent to muscles, telling them to react.

Review the fact that there are 31 pairs of nerves that branch out from the spinal cord and go to all parts of the body. These are called *lateral nerves*. Lateral nerves either send signals to the spinal cord and on to the brain or receive messages to carry out in the body. Lateral nerves attach to the spinal cord at two places--a dorsal spot and ventral spot.

Review the terms dorsal (toward the back) and ventral (toward the front). Messages are carried to the brain through the dorsal connection. Messages are carried from the brain through the ventral connection. Have your student point to or trace these areas on his body.

What to Expect:

Your student should be able to make some judgments about his partner's reaction time. He should also understand the general process of how messages are transmitted to and from the brain through the spinal cord. He should be familiar with terms such as ventral, dorsal, and lateral but does not need to define them.

ASSESS

Lesson Assessment: Spinal Cord and Nerves (*Online*)

Students will complete an offline assessment based on the lesson objectives. Print the assessment and have students complete it on their own. Use the answer key to score the assessment, and then enter the results online. The attached answer key is the most current and may not coincide with previously printed guides.

Lesson Assessment

Spinal Cord and Nerves

Answers:

1. Answers may vary but should include: Bones called vertebrae protect the spinal cord from injury.

2. Read the steps below about how a reflex occurs. Circle the step or steps that do not belong.

    A. Sense receptors react to something, such as touching something hot.

    B. A nerve ending is stimulated and sends a signal up a nerve.

    C. The signal enters the spinal cord through a dorsal connection.

     D. The signal is sent to the brain and interpreted.

    E. A message is sent to the muscles.

    F. The muscles are stimulated and move in response.

3. Answers may vary but should include: Signals are sent through the nerves to the spinal cord. The spinal cord then sends these signals to the brain. Once the brain interprets the signals, it makes a decision. The brain then sends a message through the spinal cord and to the muscles, which respond to the message.

Learning Coach Guide
Lesson 7: Endocrine System: Glands and Hormones

The production of hormones is the main job of the endocrine system. Hormones are chemicals that are made in one part of the body but affect another part. Some of the most important body functions, such as the regulation of stress, are controlled by the endocrine system.

Lesson Objectives

- Identify the major glands in the endocrine system and describe their functions.
- Describe how glands and their hormones affect body processes.
- State that the endocrine system is made up of glands and hormones that function over different amounts of time.

PREPARE

Approximate lesson time is 60 minutes.

Materials

For the Student
- 🖥 The Endocrine System
- 🖥 Feedback Mechanisms

For the Adult
- 🖥 The Endocrine System Answer Key
- 🖥 Feedback Mechanisms Answer Key

Lesson Notes

In this lesson, another system will be introduced--the *endocrine system*. It is in charge of many bodily functions, including the response to danger. If your student has ever felt a sudden surge of energy and an increased heart rate at being frightened, he has experienced one of the effects of the endocrine system.

- The endocrine system is composed of nine glands, each of which produces a special chemical known as a *hormone*. Some glands produce more than one hormone.

Hormones travel though the blood stream. When they arrive at special cells, called *target cells*, receptors on the cells recognize them. The hormone and the target cell attach to each other, and changes in the body are kicked off.

When a gland receives stimulation through a command from the brain, cells inside it produce a specific hormone. The gland then secretes the hormone into the blood. Glands put hormones directly into the bloodstream, rather than having ducts or tubes that connect them to blood vessels.

The Adrenal Gland

The adrenal glands are located on the kidneys. "Ad" means *on top of* and "renal" means *kidney*. Each gland has two parts: the *cortex* and the *medulla*.

The Thyroid Gland

Another gland, the *thyroid*, produces *thyroxine*. This hormone helps in the regulation of body chemistry.

The Pituitary Gland

Probably the single most important gland in the body is the *pituitary*. The pituitary gland is located in the base of the brain next to the hypothalamus. Special nerves connect them, and the hypothalamus secretes various chemicals into the pituitary gland. The two structures work together. The pituitary gland has two major sections, called *lobes*. There is an anterior lobe and a posterior lobe.

Islets of Langerhans

Insulin is a hormone that regulates sugar levels in the body. It is made in the pancreas, in structures called the *Islets of Langerhans*.

Insulin lowers the amount of sugar in the blood by letting it enter cells. If a person has too much insulin, too little sugar may be in the blood. This condition is called *hypoglycemia*. And, if insulin isn't being produced properly, a person may suffer from a form of *diabetes*. Diabetes is a serious disease, but can be controlled with medications and diet, or in some cases treated with insulin injections.

Keywords and Pronunciation

adrenal (uh-DREE-nl)

adrenaline (uh-DREH-nl-uhn)

cretinism (KREE-tn-ih-zuhm)

endocrine (EN-duh-kruhn)

endocrine system (EN-duh-kruhn) : A body system made up of glands and hormones that work with the nervous system. The endocrine system is one of the body's control systems.

gland : An organ that produces chemicals that perform special jobs in the body. The thyroid gland produces a chemical called thyroxine.

hormone : A chemical produced by glands and released into the bloodstream. Hormones are produced in one part of the body but affect a different part.

hypoglycemia (hiy-poh-gliy-SEE-mee-uh)

islets of Langerhans (IY-luhts of LAHNG-uhr-hahnts)

medulla : One of two tissue types found in the adrenal glands. This tissue is reponsible for producing adrenaline and noradrenaline.

pancreas (PAN-kree-uhs)

pituitary (puh-TOO-uh-tair-ee) : A gland found at the base of the brain, responsible for making human growth hormone. The pituitary gland is the main gland responsible for growth.

thyroxine (thiy-RAHK-seen)

TEACH
Activity 1: Glands at Work *(Online)*

Instructions

Have your student read through the Explore on his own. Reinforce and explain difficult concepts as needed.

Explore Suggestions:

Screen 3: Review by having your student point to areas of his body that contain the following glands and organs:

- Adrenal (lower back, kidneys)
- Pituitary (lower back of head)
- Thyroid (throat)
- Pancreas (stomach)
- Brain (head)

After this activity, check to see if your student can do the following:

After this activity, check to see if your student can do the following:

- State that the endocrine system is made up of glands and hormones that function over different amounts of time.
- Identify the major glands in the endocrine system and describe their functions.
- Describe how glands and their hormones affect body processes.

If your student has difficulty with any of these concepts, you may wish to review the Explore with him and have him explain the key points on each screen.

Safety

As usual, you may wish to preview the websites listed in this lesson.

Note: the website suggested in this activity has a reference to the reproductive glands.

Activity 2: The Great Regulator: The Endocrine System (Offline)

Instructions

Teaching:

Your student may use the Explore section to complete this activity.

What to Expect:

Your student should be able to identify the major glands of the endocrine system and use the Explore text to fill in the blanks correctly.

Answers:

See the Endocrine System Answer Key.

Activity 3: Feedback Mechanisms: Message Received (Offline)

Instructions

Teaching:

Review the role of the endocrine system in the body. The endocrine system is responsible for the regulation of certain conditions of the body. These include water concentration in cells, growth, blood sugar levels, and responses to fear. Glands that respond to changes in the body accomplish this. Endocrine glands secrete chemical messages, called *hormones*. The hormones activate responses in parts of the body, achieving regulation. This process is called a *feedback mechanism*. This activity discusses the role of hormones and specific responses. Three examples of feedback mechanisms are provided.

What to Expect:

Your student should understand the role of the pancreas and hypothalamus in secreting hormones and regulating water concentration, blood sugar levels, and body temperature. He should be able to describe the role of each hormone in the first two processes.

Answers:

See the Feedback Mechanisms Answer Key.

ASSESS

Lesson Assessment: Endocrine System: Glands and Hormones (Online)

Students will complete an online assessment based on the lesson objectives. The assessment will be scored by the computer. The attached answer key is the most current and may not coincide with previously printed guides.

Name _____   Date _____

The Endocrine System Answer Key

Use the word box to label the main glands of the endocrine system. Then fill in the blanks to describe their functions.

brain

pituitary gland

Word Box
Word Box brain adrenal glands thyroid pituitary gland pancreas

thyroid

adrenal glands

pancreas

1. Insulin, a hormone that regulates sugar uptake, is produced in the
   _____**pancreas**_____.

2. This gland, called the _____**thyroid**_____, makes thyroxine,
   which is involved in growth.

3. The _____**pituitary gland**_____ is often called the "*master gland*"
   because it produces so many different hormones.

4. The organ that gives orders to glands to release hormones is the
   _____**brain**_____.

5. Located on the kidneys, the _____**adrenal glands**_____ make adrenaline,
   which helps the body respond to fear.

Name _____   Date _____

Feedback Mechanisms

For you to carry out normal activities, certain factors inside your body must be regulated. These are things such as temperature, blood sugar, and water. It's dangerous for your body to get too hot, too cold, or too dry on the inside.

Your body stays regulated with the help of receptors and effectors. Receptors sense when something changes in your body. Effectors respond to the change. In other words, receptors send the message. Effectors say, "Message received!" and respond as needed. This process of sensing changes and adjusting to them is called a *feedback mechanism*. The levels of hormones in the body are controlled by feedback mechanisms.

Why are feedback mechanisms important? They are necessary for survival. If you step outside on a very cold day, a feedback mechanism keeps your internal body temperature high. Feedback mechanisms help you adjust to a change in your environment.

Let's take a look at how some feedback mechanisms regulate your body.

Feedback Mechanisms

Water Regulation

Your cells need a certain amount of water to carry out cell processes. Trace the path of this feedback mechanism below on the diagram.

- Receptors that detect changes in water concentration are located on the hypothalamus.
- A change in water concentration activates these receptors.
- The hypothalamus sends a message to the pituitary gland next to it.
- The pituitary gland puts out a hormone (ADH) that targets the kidneys.
- Then ADH gets to the kidneys. It causes changes, making the kidneys able to take in more or less water (as needed).
- A little ADH makes the kidneys take in less water to be released in the blood stream.
- Concentrated ADH makes the kidneys take in more water to be released in the blood stream.

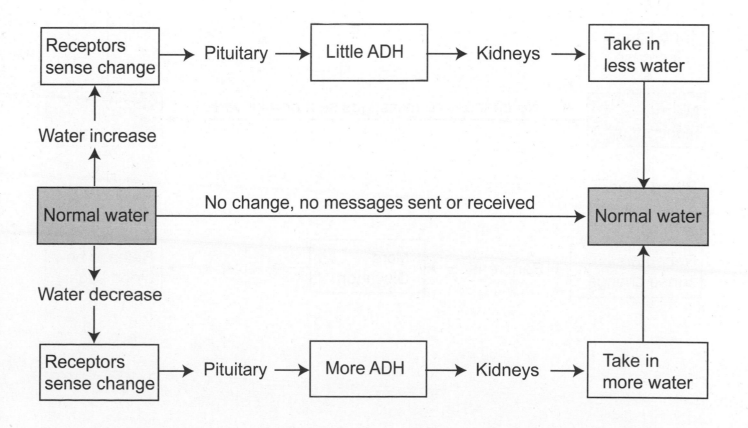

Feedback Mechanisms

Blood Sugar Regulation

Your body needs certain levels of blood sugar to make energy. There are two hormones responsible for regulating blood sugar: insulin and glucagon. Trace the path of this feedback mechanism below on the diagram.

- A change in blood sugar switches on receptors in the pancreas.
- The pancreas puts out two types of hormones: insulin and glucagon.
- More insulin is released when blood sugar levels are high.
- More glucagon is released when blood sugar levels are low.
- Insulin and glucagon affect the liver.
- Insulin will cause the liver to store blood sugar instead of release it. Glucagon will cause the liver to produce new blood sugar and release it to cells.

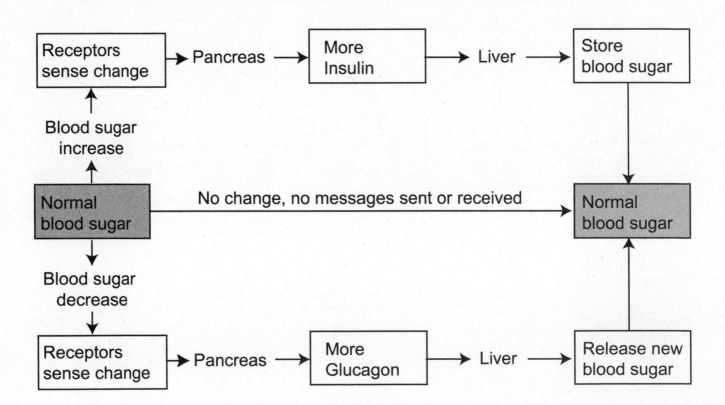

Feedback Mechanisms Answer Key

Temperature Regulation

Mammals and birds are able to regulate their body temperatures to adapt to their environments. This means that when they get too hot, their bodies react to cool them down. When they are too cold, their bodies respond in ways to keep them warm.

Read the steps involved in temperature regulation. Then, fill in the diagram.

- A change in temperature (increase or decrease) is sensed by receptors in the skin.
- The skin sends this information to the hypothalamus.
- The hypothalamus sends nerve impulses to the body.
- If the body is too hot, heat is released by sweating and by widening the blood vessels.
- If the body is too cold, heat is trapped by shivering, by tightening the blood vessels, and by making the hair stand on end.

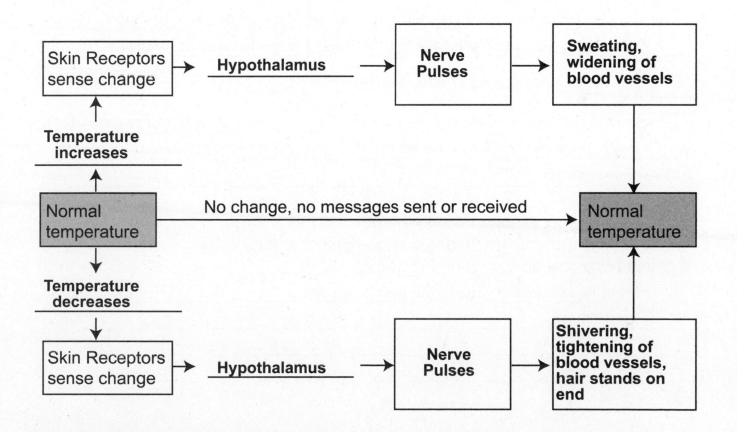

Feedback Mechanisms Answer Key

Review and Questions

Regulated levels of water, blood sugar, and temperature are necessary for your survival. Feedback mechanisms tell the body how to act by sending and receiving messages that bring about a response. Hormones are often very important in this process.

1. Tell which gland the following hormones come from.

   ADH _____**Pituitary**_____

   Insulin ____**Pancreas**_____

   Glucagon **Pancreas**_____

2. Describe how each hormone keeps conditions of the body regulated.

   ADH ___**ADH helps regulate water concentration. A little ADH makes the kidney**___
   _____**take in less water. Concentrated ADH makes the kidney take in more**___
   _____**water.**_____

   Insulin __**Insulin helps regulate blood sugar levels. If blood sugar is too high,**___
   _____**insulin will cause the liver to store blood sugar instead of release it.**___
   _____

   Glucagon ___**Glucagon helps regulate blood sugar levels, also. If blood sugar is too**___
   _____**low, glucagon will cause the liver to produce and release more blood**___
   _____**sugar.**_____

3. Diabetes is a condition in which there is too much sugar in the blood. People who suffer from diabetes take injections of a certain hormone. Which hormone do you think they take? Why?

   _____**Insulin, because it causes the liver to store**_____
   _____**blood sugar.**_____
   _____
   _____

Learning Coach Guide
Lesson 8. Optional: Growing Up

Your student may be concerned about growing up and the changes he will go through. But, in fact, he is already doing it. In this lesson he will begin to understand how the pituitary gland from the endocrine system controls this process.

Lesson Objectives

- Describe how the pituitary gland affects human growth.
- Describe aspects of a career in neuroscience.

PREPARE

Approximate lesson time is 60 minutes.

Materials

For the Student

paper, ruled

pencil

Lesson Notes

Your student is right in the midst of a powerful natural process--physical growth. While what is commonly meant by "grow up"! is a change in behavior, your student is also involved in quite literal, physical changes. These changes will become even more dramatic at puberty. For most people puberty occurs between the ages of 11 and 14. This is not always the case, though.

In its largest sense, growth is always happening. It begins the day we are born--indeed, before we are born-- and continues until we die. The most extreme changes, though, happen to us when we are young. The main cause of these changes is hormones.

Hormones

Hormones control:

- the growth of bones
- the fusing together of bones
- the change from cartilage to bone

Indeed, most growth is controlled by the endocrine system.

Pituitary Gland

The pituitary gland in particular plays a central role in growth. The pituitary has two lobes, known as the *anterior lobe* and the *posterior lobe*. The anterior lobe produces six hormones, all of which contribute to growth. The most important is *human growth hormone*, or HGH.

Genetics and Disorders

Height and weight are inherited characteristics. They are largely determined by genes that are passed to us from our parents. As parents have the gene that they then pass to their children, children often resemble their parents.

Some people have pituitary disorders, which cause changes in height and size. In different communities in the world, however, very different standards of height and size are considered normal. Andre the Giant and others are merely presented in the lesson to show how powerfully the pituitary gland, and HGH in particular, affect the body.

Keywords and Pronunciation

acromegaly (a-kroh-MEH-guh-lee) : A disease that causes excess growth. Andre the Giant was a wrestler who suffered from acromegaly.

cartilage (KAHR-tl-ij)

endocrine (EN-duh-kruhn)

pituitary (puh-TOO-uh-tair-ee) : A gland found at the base of the brain, responsible for making human growth hormone. The pituitary gland is the main gland responsible for growth.

puberty : A process controlled by the endocrine system in which changes occur in the body. Puberty usually occurs between the ages of 11 and 14.

TEACH
Activity 1. Optional: Optional Lesson Instructions (Offline)

Activity 2. Optional: How You Grow (Online)
Instructions
Have your student read through the Explore on his own. Reinforce and explain difficult concepts as needed.
Explore Suggestions:
Screen 5: If you have a family photo available, have your student compare how the members of his family look alike.
After this activity, check to see if your student can:
   • Describe how the pituitary gland affects human growth.
If your student has difficulty with any of these concepts, you may wish to review the Explore with him and have him explain the key points on each screen.

Activity 3. Optional: Measuring Up (Online)
Instructions
Teaching:
Review the role of the pituitary gland in growth. This gland secretes a human growth hormone, or HGH, that instructs the body in several ways. HGH instructs cells to divide, making our bodies grow. HGH and genes play a role in how tall or short we are. Genes inherited from parents will determine our eventual height.
Troubleshooting:
If your student is insecure about being taller or shorter than peers or friends, explain that our bodies and theirs are still growing. The final changes to our height don't happen until we are young adults. Very tall kids may find others growing tall around them. Short kids may find themselves growing taller as they become teenagers.
What to Expect:
Your student should understand how his height ranks among other children his age. He should also understand that his height is determined by genes and human growth hormone, secreted by the pituitary gland.

Activity 4. Optional: Careers in Medicine *(Online)*

Instructions

Teaching:

Discuss the fact that the discoveries and advances made in science would not have been possible without the dedicated research of doctors and scientists. Add to the career possibilities your student may already have by discussing neuroscience.

Troubleshooting:

Although the website used is written for children, some of the terms may be unfamiliar and challenging to your student.

What to Expect:

Your student should understand the major duties and training involved in a career in neuroscience. Look for the following in his report:

- A description of an education path that involves college, graduate school, research, and experience in a lab setting.
- A description of a day in the life of a neuroscientist that involves the many roles a neuroscientist plays.
- A description of what future research your student would like to do based on those presented on the website.
- A description of a logical challenge in working in neuroscience. Your student may have to come up with this idea on his own.
- Advice your student thinks should be given to someone considering a career in this field. May be something such as "Study hard in school" or the like.

Learning Coach Guide
Lesson 9. Optional: Daily Processes and Hormones

Hormones help control many daily processes. They help manage blood sugar levels, how we sleep, and even tell us when we are hungry. Your student will explore the different stages of the sleep-wake cycle and digestion, and learn about the relationship between the disease called *diabetes* and the hormone *insulin*.

Lesson Objectives

- Recognize that hormones play a role in controlling daily bodily processes like blood-glucose regulation, hunger, digestion, and the sleep-wake cycle.
- Explain how insulin and glucagon act in the regulation of blood sugar.
- Explain how abnormalities in the hormone insulin, or in its use by the cells in the body, can cause diabetes.
- Describe the stages of the sleep-wake cycle.

PREPARE

Approximate lesson time is 60 minutes.

Materials

For the Student

household item - clock

paper, ruled

pencil

Lesson Notes

Our bodies store the energy we get from food and let us use it a little at a time. Although it may be surprising to your student, our bodies also signal us to know when to get hungry. This process is controlled by hormones. So are other basic processes, such as knowing when to sleep and when to wake up.

Strange as it may sound, scientists do not know exactly why we sleep. If sleep only fills our need for bodily rest, then sitting quietly in a chair should be sufficient. But we know that sleep is necessary for health. Research shows that sleep-deprived people have trouble with tasks such as problem solving and thought processing.

- People tend to sleep about 8 hours a night--roughly a third of our lives.

Human sleep is divided into five stages that are based on electrical activity in the brain. This activity can be monitored by electrode sensors, which can be attached to sleeping person's head.

- The first four stages are called slow-wave sleep (SWS).
- The fifth stage is called rapid eye movement sleep (REM).

During *REM sleep,* the sleeper's eyes move around in rapid jumps. People experience dreams the most during REM sleep.

When we sleep we go through four SWS stages, and then through a period of REM sleep. A whole sleep cycle lasts about 100 minutes, with REM sleep taking about only 10 minutes.

The hormones prostaglandin D2, adenosine, and melatonin are some of many chemical messengers that encourage your body to sleep. Melatonin is released by the pineal gland especially at night. The pineal gland is light sensitive, so it can become used to to the rising and setting of the sun.

Like sleep, hunger is stimulated by hormones:

- *Orexin* is a recently discovered hormone in the hypothalamus, and is related to hunger.
- *Ghrelin* stimulates hunger when the stomach is empty.
- CCK and PYY3-36 in the intestines decrease hunger when the intestines are full.
- *Leptin* is produced by fat cells, and decreases hunger.

The body's energy is largely a matter of blood sugar. When blood sugar is low, the pancreas puts the hormone *glucagon* into the blood. Receiving the glucagon signal, the liver turns some glycogen into blood sugar, putting it in the bloodstream so cells everywhere can use it.

When glucose levels are high in the blood, the pancreas makes insulin. Insulin signals the liver to change some blood sugar into glycogen. The glycogen can be stored for later use.

Keywords and Pronunciation

adenosine (uh-DEE-nuh-seen)

ghrelin (GREH-lin)

glucagon (GLOO-kuh-gahn)

glycogen (GLIY-kuh-juhn)

insulin : A hormone produced in the pancreas that helps regulate blood-sugar levels. Our cat Patches has feline diabetes, so each morning I help my mother give him an insulin shot.

melatonin (meh-luh-TOH-nuhn)

orexin (uh-REHK-sin)

pancreas (PAN-kree-uhs)

pineal (PIY-nee-uhl)

prostaglandin (prahs-tuh-GLAN-duhn)

TEACH
Activity 1. Optional: Optional Lesson Instructions *(Offline)*

Activity 2. Optional: Some Daily Dealings with Hormones *(Online)*
Instructions

Have your student read through the Explore on his own. Reinforce and explain difficult concepts as needed.

Explore Suggestions:

Screen 1: Have your student think back to what he has eaten so far today. Ask him to name some of the activities that the food energy has helped him do.

After this activity, check to see if your student can:

[A] Recognize that hormones play a role in controlling daily processes like blood glucose regulation, hunger, digestion, and the sleep-wake cycle.

[B] Explain how insulin and glucagon act in regulation of blood sugar.

[C] Explain how abnormalities in the hormone insulin or in its use by the cells in the body can cause diabetes.

[D] Describe the stages of the sleep-wake cycle.

If your student has difficulty with any of these concepts, you may wish to review the Explore with him and have him explain the key points on each screen.

Activity 3. Optional: Sleep Experiments (Online)
Instructions
Teaching:

The average person sleeps about 8 hours a day. This allows us to go through several cycles in our sleep. Each cycle begins with the four stages of SWS and ends with REM sleep. REM sleep is the stage in the sleep-wake cycle in which we dream.

Your student will be asked to keep a sleep journal to find out about his sleep patterns. He will need a clock by his bedside for a week to record the time he goes to bed and when he wakes up each day. He should record the times he was dreaming right before he woke up. This would mean that he woke up during the REM sleep stage of the cycle. Encourage your student to discuss any dreams he may have had.

Troubleshooting:

If your student is having a hard time keeping track of his sleep patterns, complete the activity yourself and share your discoveries with him each day.

What to Expect:

Most kids go through about four or five different cycles while they sleep.

Activity 4. Optional: Dealing with Diabetes (Online)
Instructions
Teaching:

Have your student visit the Juvenile Diabetes Research Foundation International to learn about some of the many people that have diabetes. The site provides information about these role models that explain some of the trials and tribulations that they go through each day as they live with the disease. After reading about some of them, your student will be asked to write about some of the things that they do to deal with their diabetes.

Troubleshooting:

If your student is having difficulty writing about some of the role models, read through a few of the articles with him and discuss what they are doing to help control their diabetes.

Learning Coach Guide
Lesson 10: Unit Review and Assessment

Your student will be asked to help solve a mystery involving some type of organism found in Dr. Finster's lab. As he does this, he will be reviewing all that he has learned about in the Human Body unit to prepare for the unit assessment.

Lesson Objectives

- Explain that the various systems of the human body function because the cells, tissues, and organs all work together.
- Describe that the brain gets information about the outside world and the rest of the body through nerves, and uses nerves to direct actions by other parts of the body.
- Define *senses, reflexes, voluntary nervous system,* and *involuntary nervous system.*
- Identify various parts of the nervous system (such as the brain, spinal cord, nerves, nerve cells, and neurotransmitters), along with their structures and functions.
- Explain that the *endocrine system* is composed of glands and chemical messengers called hormones, and they function over a wide range of time scales.
- Identify locations of some major glands of the endocrine system (for example, adrenals, thyroid, pituitary, pancreas).
- Define a body system as cells, tissues and organs working together to perform a certain job.
- Describe the five senses and their related sensory organs.
- Compare the voluntary nervous system with the involuntary nervous system.
- Define a reflex as movements that happen very quickly without your thinking about them.
- Identify the parts of a neuron and their functions.
- Name the three main parts of the brain: the cerebrum, cerebellum and brain stem.
- State that the spine protects the spinal cord.
- Identify the major glands in the endocrine system and describe their functions.

PREPARE

Approximate lesson time is 60 minutes.

TEACH
Activity 1: The Mysterious Organism *(Online)*
Instructions

Have your student read through the Explore on his own. Reinforce and explain difficult concepts as needed. He should answer the questions, and do the requested activities in his Science Notebook. This will be his review for the Unit Assessment. If he is having difficulty remembering any of the concepts, have him go back and review the lessons in the unit.

Explore Suggestions:

Screen 2: If your student is having difficulty drawing and labeling the parts of an animal cell, refer to screen 2 in Lesson 1, Working Together.

Screen 3: Have your student review the major parts of the nervous system. He should be able to identify the brain, spinal cord, nerves, nerve cells, and neurotransmitters as well as discuss their structures and functions. If he is having difficulty remembering the various parts, have him look back at Lessons 2 and 3, Under Control and Nerves.

Screen 4: To review reflexes, and the voluntary/involuntary activities, look back at Lesson 2, Under Control.

Screen 5: Have your student practice identifying the major glands in the endocrine system by reviewing Lesson 7, The Endocrine System: Glands and Hormones. Have him locate the pancreas, adrenal, thyroid, and pituitary glands.

After this activity, check to see if your student can:

A. Explain that the various systems of the human body function because the cells, tissues, and organs all work together.

B. Describe that the brain gets information about the outside world and the rest of the body through nerves, and uses nerves to direct actions by other parts of the body

C. Define *senses, reflexes, voluntary nervous system,* and *involuntary nervous system*.

D. Identify various parts of the nervous system (such as the brain, spinal cord, nerves, nerve cells, and neurotransmitters), along with their structures and functions.

E. Explain that the *endocrine system* is composed of glands and chemical messengers called *hormones,* which function, over a wide range of time scales.

F. Identify locations of some major glands of the endocrine system (for example, adrenals, thyroid, pituitary, pancreas).

If your student has difficulty with any of these concepts, you may wish to review the Explore with him and have him explain the key points on each screen.

ASSESS
Unit Assessment: Unit Review and Assessment: The Mysterious Organism
(*Offline*)

Students will complete this part of the Unit Assessment offline. Print the assessment and have students complete it on their own. Use the answer key to score the assessment, and then enter the results online. The attached answer key is the most current and may not coincide with previously printed guides.

TEACH
Activity 2. Optional: ZlugQuest Measurement *(Online)*

Name _____   Date _____

The Human Body Unit Assessment Answer Key

Complete questions 1-6 using the words in the Word Bank below.
Some words may be used more than once or not at all.

Word Bank

glands	cells	involuntary	
body system	voluntary	reflex	
tissue	nerves	senses	hormones

1. The building blocks of life are called _____**cells**_____. Two or more of these building blocks make up _____**tissue**_____. Organs are made from two or more kinds of _____**tissue**_____. Two or more organs make up a __**body system**__ that performs a certain job.

2. The endocrine system is made up of different _____**glands**_____, which produce chemical messengers called __**hormones**_____.

3. When it is cold outside, your body may start to shiver without your thinking about it. Shivering is an example of a _____**reflex**_____ .

4. We learn about what the world around us looks, feels, sounds, smells, and tastes like by using our five _____**senses**_____.

5. The _____**voluntary**_____ nervous system involves actions that you can control, such as deciding when to move your arm to pick up a ball. Sneezing or getting goose bumps are part of your _____**involuntary**_____ nervous system and cannot be controlled.

6. The brain gets information about the outside world and the rest of the body through _____**nerves**_____, which are made up of axons, cell bodies, and dendrites.

The Human Body Unit Assessment Answer Key

Several glands make up the endocrine system. Label the pancreas, adrenal, pituitary, and thyroid glands on the picture below.

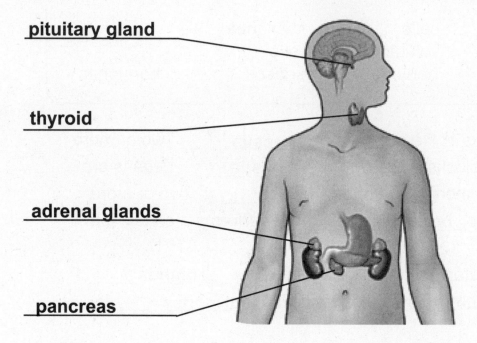

pituitary gland

thyroid

adrenal glands

pancreas

The Human Body Unit Assessment Answer Key

The words in the Word Bank below are the parts of the nervous system.
Use them to label the picture.

Word Bank

brain	cerebellum	cerebrum	brain stem	spinal cord
nerves	nerve cell	axon	dendrite	cell body
	hypothalamus		hormone	

cerebrum

brain

brain stem

cerebellum

spinal cord

cell body

nerves

nerve cell

dendrites

axon

The Human Body Unit Assessment Answer Key

Choose an item from the box below that matches each description. Then write it on the line provided.

Word Bank

brain	cerebellum	cerebrum	brain stem
spinal cord	nerves	nerve cells	axon
cell body	frontal lobe	hormones	dendrite

__nerve cells__ These are all over the body. They make up the nervous system and send messages to the brain.

__cerebellum__ This part of your brain helps you keep your balance.

__spinal cord__ It is a bundle of axons that runs up and down the back. It is covered and protected by the vertebrae.

__dendrites__ These branch-like extensions carry nerve signals toward the cell body. There are usually many of them in each cell.

__brain__ It is the control center of the human body. It is made up of three main parts: the brain stem, cerebellum, and the cerebrum.

__axon__ This carries nerve signals away from the cell body.

__brain stem__ This controls basic functions such as breathing, heart rate, and pulse.

__nerves__ Transmits signals through these to the spinal cord or brain back to the body.

__cerebrum__ It controls your thinking and reasoning.

__cell body__ This central part of the neuron contains the nucleus.

Learning Coach Guide
Lesson 11: Semester Review and Assessment

Your student will take review concepts and skills learned during the semester and then take the first Semester Assessment.

Lesson Objectives

- Identify behaviors as innate or learned.
- Describe ways to separate solutions, such as evaporation, chromatography, and distillation.
- Describe how nutrients are continuously recycled through an ecosystem among producers, consumers, and decomposers.
- Describe how water continuously moves through the water cycle as it evaporates, condenses, and precipitates.
- Recognize ways in which organisms in a community compete for food, water, and space.
- Define a *solvent* as the substance that dissolves a solute to make a solution.
- Recognize that increasing the temperature of a solvent can change the solubility of a solid solute.
- Recognize that not all substances dissolve in a given quantity of water in the same amounts.
- Describe how glands and their hormones affect body processes.
- Describe that the brain gets information about the outside world and the rest of the body through nerves, and uses nerves to direct actions by other parts of the body.
- Identify various parts of the nervous system (such as the brain, spinal cord, nerves, nerve cells, and neurotransmitters), along with their structures and functions.
- Identify locations of some major glands of the endocrine system (for example, adrenals, thyroid, pituitary, pancreas).
- Recognize examples of populations, communities, and ecosystems.
- State that sunlight is the major source of energy for ecosystems, and describe how its energy is passed from organism to organism in food webs.
- Explain how producers and consumers (herbivores, carnivores, omnivores, and decomposers) are related in food chains and food webs in an ecosystem.
- Describe how immigration and emigrations affect the size of a population.
- Define solubility as the maximum total amount of a solid that can dissolve into a given quantity of a particular solvent at a given temperature.
- Recognize that cycles in nature provide organisms with the food, air, and water they need to live, grow, and reproduce.
- State that a *population* is a group of individuals of the same type living in a certain area.
- Identify birth and immigration as the two main factors that cause an increase in a population.
- Identify death and emigration as the two main factors that cause a decrease in a population.
- Identify symbiotic relationships between organisms (mutualism, commensalism, and parasitism).
- Define *mutualism* as an interaction between two organisms in which both benefit from the relationship.
- Define a *solution* as a mixture in which the substances are completely and evenly mixed down to their individual molecules.
- Identify solute and solvents in different solutions.

- Recognize that increasing the temperature of a solvent usually increases the rate at which a solute dissolves.
- Identify the major glands in the endocrine system and describe their functions.
- Demonstrate mastery of important knowledge and skills learned this semester.
- State that the endocrine system is made up of glands and hormones that function over different amounts of time.

PREPARE

Approximate lesson time is 60 minutes.

TEACH

Activity 1: Semester Review (Online)

Instructions

Have your student read through the Semester Review. Reinforce and explain difficult concepts as needed. Revisit any specific lessons your student found difficult during the semester.

ASSESS

Semester Assessment: Science 4, Semester 1 (Offline)

Students will complete an offline Semester assessment. Print the assessment and have students complete it on their own. Use the answer key to score the assessment, and then enter the results online. The attached answer key is the most current and may not coincide with previously printed guides.

Name _____   Date _____

Semester Assessment Answer Key

Read each question and circle the letter next to the correct answer.

1. Yucca moths lay eggs in yucca flowers. When the eggs hatch, the larvae eat yucca seeds. The moths help pollinate the flowers. What type of symbiosis is this?

   (A) mutualism

   B. commensalism

   C. parasitism

2. Chemical messengers in the endocrine system carry signals to organs and glands to respond to bodily changes. What are these messengers called?

   A. homunculus

   (B) hormones

   C. tissues

   D. cells

3. When an organism dies, what happens to the nutrients that have been transferred to it?

   A. The nutrients are lost.

   (B) The nutrients are recycled back to the soil.

   C. The nutrients are multiplied.

   D. The nutrients cause the organism to rot and decay.

4. Imagine you see a famous person. Which best explains the process of how your nervous system "senses" the person, then instructs you to ask for an autograph?

   A. eyes – spinal cord - brain – spinal cord – nerves in mouth

   B. eyes – spinal cord – nerves in mouth

   (C) eyes – brain – mouth

   D. brain – eyes – nerves in mouth

Semester Assessment Answer Key

TRUE or FALSE. If the statement is false, correct it.

5. (Two point Question) Once water and air are used by an organism, they are lost to the environment forever.
   A. True   **Once water and air are used by an organism, they**
   (B) False   **are recycled back into the environment.**

6. (Three point question) Match the method of how to separate solutions to its description.

Evaporation

Distillation

Paper chromatography

A solvent is used to separate colors in a solution on an absorbent paper.

The solution is boiled and the solute remains behind.

A solution is poured through a strainer to seperate large particles

The solution is boiled and the evaporated liquid is collected while the solute remains.

Semester Assessment Answer Key

Fill in the blanks with words from the Word Bank to complete the sentences.

solvent	population	solute	immigration
emigration solution		gram	community

7. A tomato plant is an individual. A group of tomato plants growing in your backyard is a __**population**__.

8. In a mixture of salt and water, both substances mix evenly, down to individual molecules. Saltwater is a ___**solution**___.

9. (Two points) Salt dissolves in water. In a mixture of saltwater, salt is the ___**solute**___ and water is the ___**solvent**___.

10. (Two points) A population of organisms changed by more organisms moving into the area is an example of __**immigration**__. A population changed by organisms moving out of the area is an example of __**emigration**__.

Semester Assessment Answer Key

11. (One point for each question) Label the brain, spinal cord, and nerves in the illustration.

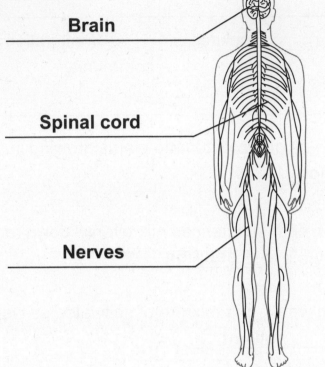

Brain

Spinal cord

Nerves

12. (One point for each question) Label the brain, adrenals, thyroid, pituitary gland, and pancreas in the illustration.

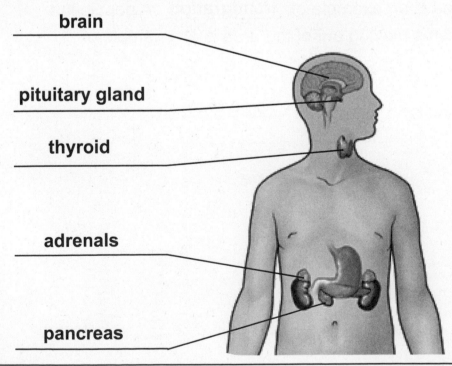

brain

pituitary gland

thyroid

adrenals

pancreas

Semester Assessment Answer Key

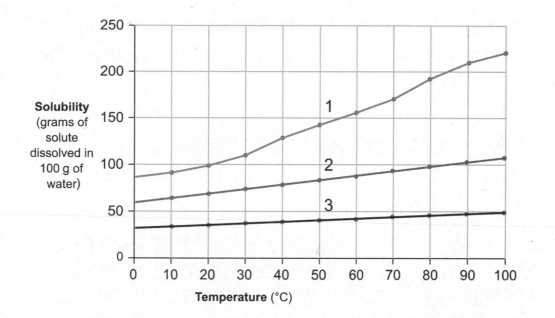

13. Write the solubility of solid 1, 2, and 3 at 50 °C. __**145 g, 80 g, 45 g**__

14. Study solid 1. What happens to its solubility as the water temperature increased? __**It becomes more soluble. More grams of it can dissolve in hotter water.**__

15. (Two points) Assume that solid 1 is sugar and solid 3 is salt. Would you expect the same amount of sugar and salt to dissolve in the same amount of water? Why or why not? __**No, because not all substances can dissolve in water in the same amounts.**__

Semester Assessment Answer Key

16. Draw a food chain containing the sun, a producer, a consumer, and a decomposer. Draw arrows to show the transfer of energy. **(3 points)**

Sample:

Sun → **Grass** → **Rabbit** → **Bacteria**

17. (Three points) Explain in writing how energy is transferred through the food chain you've drawn. **The producer uses energy from the sun for photosynthesis. The consumer receives some of the sun's energy by eating the producer. When organisms die, energy Is then transferred to a decomposer that breaks down the organisms body into nutrients.**

18. Name an example of parasitism. **Any example in which one organism benefits and another is harmed. Example: Tapeworms living in the intestines of animals.**

19. Name one learned behavior and one innate behavior. **Any example of learned behavior such as training a dog and any example of innate behavior such as newborn ducks knowing how to swim.**

20. Explain the difference between a population, a community, and an ecosystem, using the hare as an example. **A group of hares is a population. A community includes the hares and other organisms around it. An ecosystem includes the hares, other organisms, and nonliving parts of the environment such as air and water.**

Semester Assessment Answer Key

21. (Two points) Name two resources a population of hares may compete for.

food, shelter, or water

22. (Two points) To answer all of these questions, your brain needed to get information about the outside world. How did your brain direct the nerves in your hand to write an answer? **The brain reads questions and thinks of answers. Then signals travel from the brain to the spinal cord, then back out to the nerves in the hand, instructing the hand to write.**